THE HISTORY
OF THE
CORNISH PORT OF HAYLE

JOHN HIGGANS

The History of the Cornish Port of Hayle

© John Higgans & John Daniel

Cover Photograph:
Hayle Estuary and Harbour from the air. © Peter Channon. All Rights Reserved.
First published in *Over Cornwall* by Peter Channon.

First published 2013

Published and produced by
St Ives Printing & Publishing Company
High Street, St Ives, Cornwall TR26 1RS UK

ISBN 978-0-948385-68-1

THE
HISTORY
OF THE
CORNISH PORT
OF HAYLE

by

John Higgans

St Ives Printing & Publishing Company

JOHN HIGGANS WAS born in Hayle in 1917, the son of Frederick and Daisy Higgans (nee West). He married Pera Clements of Boughton Aluph in Kent in 1945 and they have two daughters.

After leaving school he was employed in the office of the Hayle Gas Company owned by Harvey & Co Ltd which he later joined in 1937 and re-established his West family connection with the company, which dates back to the 18th Century, with the marriage in 1784 of William West to Joanna Harvey, a daughter of John Harvey who established the Foundry in Hayle in 1779.

John Higgans served in the Royal Artillery from 1939 to 1946 when he rejoined Harvey & Co Ltd. He qualified as a Chartered Secretary in 1947 and was appointed his employer's Company Secretary in 1948 and later a Director in 1960. He held these positions until his retirement in 1975.

The main interest of John Higgans at school was English history which later developed into local and family history on which he wrote many articles which appeared in the journals of the Old Cornwall and Cornwall Family History Societies. In 1986 he published his history of Angarrack, Hayle from whence his father's ancestors emigrated to Australia in 1848.

In 1975 John Higgans and his wife moved from Hayle to Newton Abbot in Devon to be nearer their daughters.

Contents

Foreword

IN 1969 UBM buys out Harvey & Company.

Harbour put up for sale and sold in 10 lots for development.

1983 – Tekoa buys the harbour and presents plans that are never agreed. Tekoa were based in Devon and were demolition experts – they removed many historic buildings and filled in parts of the Carnsew Dock.

In 1988 Peter de Savery (Aldersgate) became involved in Hayle, taking over from Tekoa and presenting some grandiose development plans. In the early 1990s he submitted a scheme for 456 houses and 1,400 square metres of shops, with 140 hectares devoted to wildlife conservation (selling parts of his holdings to the RSPB). The first phase was land reclamation. The scheme also included the construction of a barrage across the estuary in order to create perpetual waterways in a 'Port Grimaud' style development. Plans were never fulfilled.

De Savery disposed of his holdings and the next developer was a company called Rosshill whose principal was a North Country businessman named Phillip Caruthers. The company promoted plans in 1998 but by 2003 became bankrupt.

One of the shareholders for the Rosshill Company was a group called London and Amsterdam, part of the ING Bank. When Caruthers went bankrupt they took over the Hayle properties creating a company called London and Amsterdam (Hayle) Ltd which became part of the ING Red property operation subsequently being set up as ING Red (Hayle Harbour) Ltd.

John Pollard
09/03/13

Preface

MUCH HAS BEEN written in books, local newspapers and journals about various aspects of Hayle's past. The history of the town's two engineering works and their proprietors – the Harveys of Foundry and the Cornish Copper Company of Copperhouse – whose products, especially their Cornish mine engines, were famous worldwide, have received most of the attention, especially in *The Harveys of Hayle* by Edmund Vale and *The History of the Cornish Copper Company* by W. H. Pascoe. Though featured in these books, the history of the Cornish port of Hayle, at one time one of the country's busiest small ports and of vital importance to the people and economy of West Cornwall, has not been chronicled in any detail.

In my quest for information to supplement the results of my research on which I have based *The History of the Port of Hayle* I have received help and suggestions from a number of persons. For their assistance it is my pleasure to thank Mr D. Burrell of Lloyd's of London; Mr Clive Carter of Sancreed, an authority on Cornwall's coastal shipping; Mr T. J. Everson of Blue Circle Industries Ltd of London; Mr A. W. Groves of the Penzance Custom House; Mr W. B. Harrison, a partner in the firm of Whitford & Sons, Harvey's solicitors for decades; Mr D. P. Harvey, a former director of Harvey & Company Ltd; Mr L. F. Johnson of the House of Lords library; Dr A. Hood of the Maritime Museum, Greenwich, the Curator , Hydrographic Department, Ministry of Defence; Mr L. F. Jenkin of Harveys Quay Company Ltd; Capt Eric Kemp and Mr T. Lander, both of St Ives; Mr David Mudd, MP; Mr W. H. Pascoe of Exmouth; Mr Brian Sullivan of Hayle for photographs and extracts from old port books owned by the late Miss A. G. D. La Touche of Hayle who kindly allowed me to use them; Mr Martin Weiler of the South West Water Authority and the directors of the UBM Group of Bristol, now a part of Norcros Plc, for allowing me to make use of the old Harvey records.

For the plan of the port of Hayle, I am indebted to Mr A. H. Kennedy, a partner in the firm of Body, Son & Fleury (now Fleury Manico), Chartered Surveyors of Plymouth. He and his firm had a very long association with Harvey & Company Ltd.

John Higgans
Newton Abbot, Devon

Introduction

IN SIMPLE TERMS a harbour is a place of refuge for ships. Its potential for development from a mere haven into a port depends on its geographical position, natural features and the extent of any commercial and industrial activity in its hinterland. The absence of a means of communication with distant parts of the country, other than by sea, is also a determining factor.

Almost completely enclosed by land, Hayle has one of the two sheltered harbours on the exposed north coast of Cornwall – Padstow having the other – and up to the middle of the last century links with other regions, apart from those by ship, were virtually non-existent.

From the beginning of the eighteenth century the growth of the tin and copper mining industries, within a few miles of Hayle, provided the economic base for its development as a seaport. All that was necessary to make good use of the opportunities to bring this about were the human qualities of enterprise and determination. It so happened, as the reader will discover in due course, that men with these virtues were at hand in the eighteenth and nineteenth centuries.

In the days when canals, turnpike roads, railways and ports were constructed the interests of the landowners, builders and users were usually in conflict. If the differences between the various parties could be resolved the work was usually undertaken under the statutory authority of an Act of Parliament which set out what could be done and where, and the tolls and dues which could be levied to meet the cost of the work and its maintenance. An attempt was made in 1801 to secure such powers of regulation to develop the port of Hayle, but it was not successful, and as a result the various stages of its development were completed in disorder – in more ways than one.

There had been some minor development of the port prior to 1756 in which year the Cornish Copper Company transferred its copper smelting operations from Camborne to Hayle so as to eliminate the cost of transporting inland the coal which it needed in large quantities. In the years that followed, the company carried out a number of schemes to aid the passage of vessels between the entrance to the harbour and its works at the eastern end of the estuary at Ventonleague. By 1800 it had gained control of all the quays in the port and had built up a thriving business with the local mines by supplying them with coal, timber, lime, iron and other materials, and storing their copper ores before shipment to South Wales where much of it was increasingly being smelted.

In the year 1779 John Harvey, a blacksmith from nearby Gwinear, built a small iron foundry at Carnsew on the southern edge of the Hayle estuary. His purpose was to make castings required for the machinery of the local mines.

As time passed the demand for these increased and John Harvey bought a small vessel, the *Providence*, to bring the coal and iron he needed for his foundry from South Wales. This little ship could not get near the foundry, even on the highest tides, and from where it lay aground at low water its cargoes had to be loaded into carts and taken ashore. In spite of these difficulties John Harvey was able to import enough coal for his own needs and to supply some to the mines in the neighbourhood. This encouraged him to do more business with them and when he attempted to do so it set him on a collision course with the Cornish Copper Company which was determined to hold on to its monopoly of the trade in port which it had recently gained. The company's opposition to the Harveys resulted, for many years, in bitter conflict between the two parties, both in the courts of law and the mud and sand of Hayle harbour. Competition between the two sides finally ended in 1867 when the Cornish Copper Company ceased business and Harvey & Company bought its waterside premises and became the sole operators in the port.

With no means of communication with the industrial parts of the country, except by sea, Hayle by the early eighteenth century became the place to which such basic commodities as coal, building materials and simple finished goods were brought in for the mines and the local domestic market. It was also the way out for the locally produced copper ore. Although coal was, and continued to be, the mainstay of the trade, the range of goods handled in the port widened as time passed. Then in 1831 came a regular packet service between Hayle and Bristol for passengers and a variety of consignments as diverse as cattle and coffee. With the coming of these packet ships, propelled by steam power, the harbour scene, so long dominated by sails, began to change.

With the closure of many of the local mines and the coming of the railways the port of Hayle might have gone into decline by the beginning of the 20th century. However, the losses sustained were more than compensated for by the requirements of a new coal burning Electric Power Station built on the edge of the harbour, an increasing demand for domestic coal, grain, building materials and the new petroleum products, petrol and oil. The need to import all these ensured that the port continued in use for another seventy years. Decline finally set in with a shift in the pattern of seaborne trade and the demise of the local industries which made use of the port.

Over the years the port of Hayle attracted the attention of a number of organisations concerned with maritime affairs. The first of them was HM Customs and, in due course, Trinity House, Lloyd's of London, the Royal National Lifeboat Institution and the Vice-Consular Service of Norway and Sweden.

The Harbour Described

THE HARBOUR OF Hayle – it takes its name from the Cornish word 'Heyl' meaning estuary – lies on the north coast of West Cornwall and the entrance to it is at the south-west corner of St Ives Bay. From this point a channel runs inland for about half a mile and then branches out to form two inlets. One tends to the south-west for almost a mile and it has an average width of a third of that distance. The other inlet, of about the same length, but much narrower, runs north-east and was known at one time as the Est Loe, from the Cornish 'Logh' meaning inlet. In due course, this was enclosed and became known as the Copperhouse or Hayle Pool.

Into the first of the two inlets runs the Hayle river which, with a length of some eight miles, rises near Nancegollan in the parish of Crowan. From ancient times the valley of this river was a source of large quantities of alluvial tin. A smaller river, hardly more than a stream, rises in the parish of Gwinear and flows through Angarrack into the Est Loe.

As a feature, the Penpol stream which runs into the harbour, is hardly worthy of notice, but it acquired an importance out of all proportion to its size. It formed the boundary between the estate of Carnsew in the parish of St Erth and Penpol in Phillack and the steps taken by the owners of Carnsew to establish the true course of the stream, and at the same time, the ownership of one of the quays, will be later described.

As Hayle harbour is a tidal one it follows that it is navigable only at certain stages of flood and ebb tides. When it was formed, countless years ago as a drowned river valley, the harbour was deep, but the depth of water has been reduced over the centuries by deposits of silt washed down by the rivers. The incoming tides added to this state as they brought in sand in suspension which dropped on to the bed of the harbour as the flow of water slowed. As a result of the action of these natural forces the original boundaries of the harbour and the width of the entrance to it have changed over the years.

There are indications that the south-western area of the Hayle estuary once extended some distance beyond St Erth bridge as about a mile to the south of it is Porthcullum. 'Porth' is the Cornish word for 'landing place' which suggests that, at some time in the very distant past, ships could sail that far. The north-eastern arm of the estuary also extended much further inland than it does now and the sea reached as far as the site where the remains of Loggans Hill now stand.

We are afforded a glimpse of what conditions were like in the Hayle estuary in 1758.(1) It was navigable in the channel of the Hayle river for small ships as far as Lelant and lighters could reach within a 'bow shot' of St Erth bridge. Ships of up to 100 tons could get into the Est Loe. Eventually sand almost filled the harbour and formed a bar at its entrance over which ships of 80 to 100 tons could pass only at the height of spring tides. The bed of the harbour was so raised that it admitted the tide in only six hours in twelve so that it flowed in the Bay three hours before it appeared in the harbour. Similar conditions applied on the ebb as the tide continued to recede in the Bay long after the last of the water had left the harbour thus making it a 'half tide haven'. In these circumstances there were many occasions when vessels could not reach the quays and they had to be loaded and unloaded where they lay aground after the tide had ebbed.

There came a time in the second half of the eighteenth century when something better than the conditions just described became necessary at Hayle to deal with the increasing seaborne traffic and methods of sluicing were devised and operated to deepen the waterways of the harbour and the entrance to it and to keep them clear of sand.

Early History

DURING THE BRONZE Age, roughly from 1600 to 400 BC, there was a great demand from Europe, Ireland and elsewhere for tin which was a constituent of bronze. At the time the main sources of tin were in West Cornwall and particularly in the beds and the valleys of the streams which watered the Hayle, Camborne and Crowan areas. The harbour at Hayle became a convenient collecting point for this tin which was carried to the estuary along two ancient trackways which converged on it, one from the east and the other from the south. Tin bound for Ireland was shipped along the coast of Cornwall and Devon and South Wales and from thence across the narrowest part of the channel to Ireland. To avoid the dangerous sea route around Land's End tin destined for the continent was carried overland to St Michael's Mount – in prehistoric times this was a much shorter distance by land than it is now – and shipped from there.

From evidence provided by archaeological finds in the district it would appear that tin was exported from Hayle to Ireland and the continent as early as 1500 BC which date could therefore mark the beginning of the use of the Hayle estuary as a port.[2]

It was in the Hayle estuary that, in about 500 AD, Christian missionaries from Ireland landed and selected centres for worship in various places in the neighbourhood. The small chapels they built were the forerunners of the parish churches. Among the missionaries was Piala in whose name the church at Phillack was originally dedicated to God.

The existence of an Iron Age fort or cliff castle at Carnsew which dominates the harbour, the finding of a hoard of Roman coins nearby in 1825 and in 1843, the discovery of a fifth century grave in the fort, all suggest that Hayle as a tin port continued as such for centuries.

In the medieval period the commercial activities in the harbour were concentrated at Lelant. In 1287 one John de Trembethow was granted the liberty of buying and selling all merchandise in the borough and port of Lannanta.[3] By 1400 the sea approaches to Lelant had become so shallow that the trade of this ancient port declined and was transferred to St Ives which vessels could reach with little difficulty. John Leland, the Antiquary, who travelled through England between 1534 and 1543 and recorded his journeys in his 'Itinerary', wrote of Lelant – 'Ther came to this place ons, the haven beying embarried and syns choked with Tynne Works, good talle ships.'

Ancient stonework is still to be seen at the edge of the water near Lelant railway station and it is possible that this formed part of the quay of the medieval port of Lelant. If this is so, then these stone remains provide the only evidence we now have that, at an early date, there was a purpose built place in the harbour where ships could berth and load and unload their cargoes.

The Decision Makers

IT WILL BECOME apparent, as this narrative unfolds, that the initiative and effort required to develop the port of Hayle, and the skills necessary to manage it came from the partners of the Cornish Copper Company and members of the Harvey family.

In its early years the principal activity of the Cornish Copper Company was the smelting of copper ore, abandoned in 1819 for iron founding and engineering which, since 1779, had been Harvey's main interest. Both concerns had an expanding and valuable mine merchanting business and the affairs of the port were, to some extent, of secondary importance. Nevertheless, the problems that its development and operation created were so unusual and constant that much time had to be devoted to them. In effect, they became 'top level' responsibility.

In the case of the Cornish Copper Company the onus lay on the managing partner as his co-partners were not actively involved in the business. With the Harveys there was much the same management structure, the principal partner exercising command.

The managing partner of the Cornish Copper Company when it carried out its major improvements in the port was John Edwards of Ludgvan who entered the service of the company at an early age. He died in 1807 and was succeeded by Joseph Carne, the son of a Penzance banker. He was a very talented man, well educated and with many interests, banking, mining and merchanting among them. He was full of good works and pious being a prominent Wesleyan Methodist and a trustee of several local chapels.(4) For all his piety he had a ruthless streak in his character as is shown by the methods he used in his various attempts to crush his rivals – the Harveys. In harness for a time with Joseph Carne was Robert Mitchell of Truro. Joseph Carne retired as managing partner in 1818 but he retained his financial stake in the company and as far as his other commitments allowed, continued to exert his influence on its affairs. After Joseph Carne came John Pool as manager and then came his son John Pool Jnr. who, by 1849, had joined the partnership of the Cornish Copper Company and remained until it ceased to trade in 1867.(5)

As for the Harveys, the first of them John, had to devote much of his time and energies in making a success of his foundry and it was left to his only surviving son, Henry, to take a hand in the port's development. In this he had not only to contend with the practical problems that arose, but also with the perpetual opposition to his efforts provided in a variety of forms by the redoubtable Joseph Carne.

Henry Harvey had none of the advantages which Joseph Carne enjoyed by virtue of his superior status, education and commercial training but, as he said of himself – 'I have always made it a rule, wherever I find myself deficient, to endeavour to make it up by industry and perseverance.'(6) With this attitude and an innate intelligence he succeeded in spite of the odds against him. Not only did Henry Harvey play his part in the development of the port of Hayle he was solely responsible, for most of his life, for its day-to-day management. Towards the end of it he was assisted by one of his nephews, Richard Trevithick, son of Richard Trevithick the celebrated inventor and engineer.(7) Henry Harvey retired in 1847 and died three years later.

In 1852, another nephew, William Harvey, took over from Richard Trevithick as mercantile manager and the responsibility for the conduct of the engineering works was given to other members of the family.

When the Harvey partnership was formed into a limited liability company in 1883, by which time it had become the sole operator in the port, Frank Harvey was appointed the commercial director. His father, William Harvey, became chairman of the new company and continued as such until his death in 1893 up to which time he paid close attention to the affairs of the port as did all those chairmen of Harveys who followed him.

Frank Harvey became chairman in 1904, a position he held until he retired in 1923 when he was followed by Francis H. Harvey to 1930 and then C. V. Wills up to 1950. He was succeeded by C. P. Harvey who had been appointed a director in 1928 and who, for many years before becoming chairman of Harvey & Company, was responsible for the affairs of the port. His son, D. P. Harvey, became a director in 1949 and took over from his father and it was during the former's tenure of office that the port's handling facilities were modernised to deal with the level of imports and exports which reached their peak during this time. C. P. Harvey retired in 1958 and was followed as chairman by V. B. Wills and later P. C. Buchanan.

Up to 1965 the very diverse activities of Harvey & Company were directed and managed by the one company. Then operations were divided among three newly formed subsidiary companies, one of which, Harveys Quay Company Ltd, was entrusted with the affairs of the port of Hayle.

The Quays and Harbour Works

IN THIS CHRONICLE mention is made, from time to time, of the landed estates of Carnsew, Penpol, Bodriggy, Ventonleague, Riviere and Lelant which border the Hayle estuary. The history of these estates is a study in itself but, for the benefit of the reader their location, at least, needs to be described before dealing with the history of the quays and harbour works which make up the port of Hayle.

The estate of Ventonleague, where the Cornish Copper Company settled in 1756, lies at the inland end of the Est Loe, or to give it its modern name, Copperhouse Pool. Westward of Ventonleague lies Bodriggy and then comes Penpol divided from Carnsew, which is in St Erth parish, by the Penpol stream. Riviere estate lies to the north of the Pool and estuary with Lelant across to the west. The location of the various estates is shown on the plan of the port on page 49.

As the port's developers needed direct access to the sea the vital area, as far as they were concerned, was the land between the high and low water marks, which is the foreshore, and the waste ground at its edges known as the wastrel.

The canals, quays and weirs were built, partly or wholly, on the harbour foreshore and there is evidence that, in granting leases of the estates adjoining it the owners exercised rights of ownership over the foreshore which they did not possess. In law, the foreshores of the county of Cornwall belong to the Duke of Cornwall by virtue of a grant to the first of them, Edward the Black Prince, in 1337. In 1864 the Duchy of Cornwall asserted its rights over its foreshores and those who claimed ownership of the quays, which had by then been built on the foreshore of Hayle harbour, were obliged to buy this land from the Duchy at considerable expense.

Most of Hayle lies in the parish of Phillack but the town does not take its name from it, which is unusual. Hayle, given its name from 'heyl', the Cornish word for the estuary nearby, developed as two separate parts – Copperhouse, at the eastern end, which owes its growth to the Cornish Copper Company and includes the estates of Ventonleague, Trevassack and Bodriggy, and Foundry at the western end where Harvey's foundry lay, with the estates of Penpol, Carnsew and Trelissick.

As a result of this separate development Hayle had two of everything – in particular, local boards, gasworks, market houses, post offices, town clocks, Wesleyan chapels and literary institutes.

When the separate ends of Hayle acquired their names is not known, but the eastern part was called Copperhouse as early as 1779.(8) Following the example of the people of Plymouth Dock who changed the name of their town

16

to Devonport in 1824, a change in that of Copperhouse was proposed in the following year according to correspondence published in the *West Briton* in May 1825. Suggested alternatives were Mining Port, Kingston-on-Hayle, Haylesea and Hayleport and a meeting was to be called to decide the matter. It is not recorded that the meeting was held but if it was those in favour of retaining the old name of Copperhouse must have won the day.

Proceeding now with a description of the various quays in the port of Hayle the first for attention is Lelant Brewery Quay.

Lelant Brewery Quay

In the chapter 'Early History' mention was made of the remains of a quay, thought to be medieval in origin, near the Lelant railway station. As the harbour silted up in the years that followed its building it became difficult for ships to reach this quay and it fell into disuse. In spite of the difficulties caused by the shallow water the old quay proved very convenient for the brewery established in Lelant about 1750.(9) To it came the coal and ingredients, such as barley needed for brewing, brought by ships which were able to reach the quay when tides were high enough. This could not have been often but sufficed for the brewery. Its quay became known as Lelant Brewery Quay.

It was not until the seventeenth century that a quay was built on the eastern side of the harbour in the parish of Phillack.

Bodriggy Quay

A lease of 1710(10) relating to the Bodriggy and Penpol estates in Phillack, which abut on to the southern side of what is now Copperhouse Pool, bears a note in a contemporary hand – 'Wharfs and keys are mentioned in this lease and it is supposed that trade was first carried on in Bodriggy about the year 1685.' A plan of part of the Bodriggy and Penpol estates and dated 1835(11) shows features marked 'Bodriggy Quay' and 'Cellars' (stores) where the War Memorial now stands between the ends of Hayle Terrace and Commercial Road. Later on the land was built up in both directions at this point to provide building plots and for road improvements and the old Bodriggy Quay was obliterated. It is very likely that this quay was built in the 1680s by Peter Pendarves who, at that time, owned Bodriggy and lived there. He was a member of the Pendarves family of Pendarves, Camborne and two of his brothers were engaged in trade, one of them, Richard, being a merchant in London and the other, Stephen, in Padstow. This was an unusual occupation at that time for sons of such an ancient landed family and it is quite possible that Peter Pendarves was similarly employed and used Bodriggy Quay and Cellars as a base for his business.

The latter part of the sixteenth century marks the beginning of copper mining in Cornwall, but another hundred years were to pass before it developed to any great extent. Among the copper mines opened up in the locality of Hayle at this time were those of Herland and Relistian in nearby Gwinear parish. The nearest copper smelting works were then in South Wales so the ores from these two mines would , no doubt, have been shipped from Bodriggy Quay as would ores from the Camborne and Redruth mines until Portreath took a share of these when a quay was built there in 1715.

Merchant Curnow's Quay

The early years of the eighteenth century witnessed the expansion of deep mining in Cornwall for tin and copper and with it the development of steam power as a more efficient means of draining water from the mines. New methods of smelting the ores were also being introduced. These events brought about an increasing demand for building materials particularly bricks, lime, timber and iron as well as coal for the pumping engines at the mines and for the furnaces of the smelting houses.

John Stephens, a very successful merchant in St Ives, realised the benefits to be gained by opening a mine merchant's business on the Hayle estuary. In addition to the facilities for shipping there were mines in the neighbourhood and a domestic market as well as the tin smelting houses at nearby Angarrack and Treloweth.

In the year 1713(12) John Stephens was able to rent two acres of land on that part of the Penpol estate which bordered on the south side of the entrance to the Est Loe near the present bridges. His lease gave him 'liberty to make, build and erect any cellars, rooms, houses, yards, wharfs, docks, keys or piers' as he thought fit. With these comprehensive powers he soon set about building his quay which later became known as Merchant Curnow's Quay when that worthy took it over along with the business which John Stephens had established. The cellars, or stores, and offices were built nearby. The quay, which was faced with flat stones of random sizes and topped with granite slabs, was later lengthened by John Stephens or his successors. For the extension slag blocks, which characterise much building work in Hayle, were used. Unless supplied by a copper smelting works nearby, which closed down in 1735 after a short life, these blocks must have come from the Cornish Copper Company established at Copperhouse in 1756. Another small quay was built by John Holman, a mariner of St Ives, in about 1746, eastward of that erected by John Stephens. This quay in due course passed to John Holman's grandson, John Tremearne, and later to John Strickland, a merchant of Gwinear, in 1766.

North Quay

One of the activities of the Hayle traders was the storage of copper ore while it awaited shipment to South Wales for smelting there rather than locally. The product of each mine had to be kept separate and for this purpose a series of low walled enclosures, called plots, were built on the quays. At times, particularly during the winter months when the movements of sailing ships were hampered by bad weather, the ore might have to remain on the quays for weeks and the need for adequate space was essential. The quay that John Stephens had built was a small one and to add to the room available, another was erected opposite on the north side of the entrance to the Est Loe on the Riviere estate. It became known as Riviere Quay and later North Quay. The first section of it was probably built in the first half of the eighteenth century and extended from time to time until it reached almost a third of a mile in length. This quay, in addition to being the longest in the port, was nearest the harbour entrance and had the benefit of the deepest water. Most of North Quay, unlike others in the port, was built on solid foundations of rock which extruded from the cliff at the back of it. A minor collapse of the quay face, where the Steampacket Hotel once stood, occurred in 1926, but apart from that, North Quay has stood the test of time and use.

For the next quay to be described we have to move back again in time and across to the southern edge of the Hayle estuary at Carnsew.

Carnsew Quay

The business established by John Stephens on the Penpol estate in 1713 continued to prosper under his successors. Among them was William Lemon who, combining exceptional abilities with a fortune made in a lucky mining venture, managed to get himself a stake in many an enterprise in Cornwall. A similar character was George Blewett, a former associate of Lemon. He built up a large and successful merchanting business based at Marazion. Seeing the opportunities which were developing at Hayle, he, too, moved in to take advantage of them. In 1758 he was able to lease land at Carnsew and soon after built a stone quay and storage sheds as near as possible to the tidal water to allow ships to come alongside his quay. To improve the passage for ships using it he also had a channel dug down to the tideway. The site of Carnsew Quay which fronts on to the Basin or Carnsew Pool is now occupied by the builders' merchant business of Jewsons.

The Canal and Copperhouse Dock

In about 1754, a works was established at Entral, near Camborne, to smelt the increasing quantities of copper ore produced by the local mines. Although conveniently near to them for the ore it was not so well placed for the receipt of the coal which was required in large quantities, about three tons of it being needed to smelt one ton of ore. The coal had to come from South Wales and was probably shipped in through Portreath and then carried to Entral in panniers slung across the backs of mules. Transport by these means was expensive and even more so if any of the coal came in via Hayle. To reduce this cost the smelters decided to seek a new site for their furnaces nearer navigable water, but as close as possible to the copper mines. In 1756 they were fortunate in being able to lease an area of land which would provide adequate space and as it abutted on the foreshore, direct access to the sea. This ideal site was on the estate of Ventonleague at the head of the eastern inlet of the Hayle estuary – the Est Loe.

New smelting furnaces were built and the partnership of smelters, later to be known as the Cornish Copper Company, was soon in business with a ship of its own to bring coal from South Wales. Though near as it was to the open sea the Est Loe was too shallow for ships to make the passage right up to Ventonleague except on the highest tides so much of the coal required had to be carried up from the ships when they lay aground after sailing as far as they could into the harbour.

As the output of the copper mines increased so did the exertions of the Cornish Copper Company and its need for more and more coal. Contrary winds and bad weather could delay incoming ships for weeks during the winter months so it was essential to keep a large stock of fuel in hand. With consumption approaching 12,000 tons a year in the late 1760s there came a time when a more expeditious and less costly method of getting the coal from the ships to the works was imperative. To improve matters the partners hit on an ambitious scheme to dig a canal in the bed of the Angarrack stream, between Ventonleague and the entrance to the Est Loe, so that vessels could reach the works at all but the lowest tides. In 1768 a lease was secured from Lady Arundell, the owner of the Riviere estate, which included the Est Loe, 'to open a canal 100 feet wide to Ventonleague from the eastern part of the key called Merchant Curnow's.'(13) This deep and wide excavation completed, the upper end of the canal – the outline of the whole may still be seen – was walled with slag blocks from the smelting works nearby, to form a dock in which ships could lay to discharge their cargoes.

To keep the canal clear of accumulations of silt, gates were installed at the lower end of the dock. By closing the gates at high water and opening them when the tide had receded a strong flow of water was created which sluiced away the sand and mud which had collected since the previous clearance.

It was a common practice to take a shortcut to Copperhouse across the river by walking on top of these sluice gates when they were closed. The *Cornish Telegraph* of 27 August 1873 reported a near fatality when a young boy fell into the water in attempting to cross over in this way. Fortunately for him, he was seen to fall in by someone who raised the alarm and he was saved from drowning.

Along the outer bank of the canal guiding posts were fixed at intervals. As the direction of the wind was not always from the right quarter for ships to use their sails when passing along the canal these markers were also used as warping posts to haul them along the waterway.

Point Quay

Where the vehicle sales lot now stands (once a petrol filling station), at the foot of Cross Street in Copperhouse, there was a small quay known as Point Quay. It was in existence as early as 1788 according to the testimony of Capt. George Lovell of Swansea who stated that in that year he took a cargo of barley to the store house on the quay.(14) By the middle of the last century the property was occupied by William Hosken, miller of Loggans, and for many years he shipped to this quay cargoes of grain from Germany and elsewhere to process at his mill.

The Floodgates and Embankment

The water impounded in the Copperhouse Dock, when released, was effective in sluicing the canal leading to it, but by the time the flow had reached the entrance to the canal the force of the water was spent and of little use in clearing sand from the outer harbour. It was the practice to try and overcome this problem by using a device called a 'devil'. This was a large block of wood into which iron spikes were driven. It was driven up and down the bed of the harbour to loosen the sand so that the outgoing tide could flush it away.(15) It is of interest to record that a similar method was used in the 1950s to loosen a particularly stubborn accumulation of sand near the ferry crossing near the entrance to the harbour.

Following the ancient custom of fertilising the land with sand and seaweed, large quantities were carted from Hayle harbour and spread on local farmland. Sand was also used as ships' ballast, but all these removals were small in relation to the amount which the tide could bring in, particularly when a gale blew from the north.

As trade in the port increased something had to be done to deepen the harbour waterways and keep them in that condition so that larger vessels could use it and small ones more often. Having seen how successful they had been with their scheme to flush the canal from the Copperhouse Dock the partners of the Cornish Copper Company decided on a similar, but far more ambitious one to improve the harbour. This was to dam the water in the eastern inlet of the estuary – the Est Loe – and release it at low water to sluice away the accumulations of sand in the harbour waterways. To bring this about it was necessary to build an embankment across the entrance to the Est Loe leaving a gap for the installation of flood gates.

Up to December 1788(16), when the Cornish Copper Company bought the Riviere estate from Lord Arundell for £880 and with it his claim to the Est Loe, the company's authority to carry out any work there was limited to maintaining the canal to the Ventonleague Dock which had been made some twenty years previously. With its purchase of Riviere – later it had to buy the foreshore rights to which the Duchy of Cornwall laid claim – the company was able to proceed with its project.

The massive embankment was built with slag blocks of which the Cornish Copper Company had a plentiful supply from its smelting works. The foundations for the walls, upon which the large and heavy floodgates were hung, were made of blocks of granite as was the paving beneath the gates. The blocks for these were cut so that they locked into one another and to give them added strength were tied with iron clamps. If coffer dams were in use in those days to keep such workings clear of water as the tide ebbed and flowed one was not used on this job. After each tide receded the workings were left full of water and they had to be cleared by means of pumps – nine of them with three men to each of them.(17) As work could be resumed only when the tide had ebbed it is likely that it went on whatever the hour if the workman could see to carry on.

The two great floodgates installed each measured some 20 feet in height and 22 feet in width with a thickness of 2½ feet. What kind of timber was used for the original gates is not known but replacements in later years were constructed of greenheart, a particularly dense grained wood and very impervious to water. With their iron works these gates weighed about 15 tons each. Getting them in position and hanging them was a complicated operation. Replacements in recent years were floated up and hung as the tide receded. It may be that the original gates were fixed in this way. On the turn of the tide the gates automatically swung and closed and the water was released through shutters fitted into them which could be raised by a simple hand operated mechanism.

It was usual to open the shutters of the floodgates after the tide had ebbed. The timing for the most effective sluicing was arrived at by trial and error a long time ago and was stoutly defended by the traditionalists when there was any suggestion that it might be suspect and was the cause of unusual silting in the harbour.

To ensure that the power of the outflow of water from its new reservoir – now the Copperhouse Pool – was applied where it was needed the Cornish Copper Company built a weir down the centre of the harbour to keep the sluice water in the shipping channel. A training wall was built along the western bank of the channel at the harbour entrance to control the flow of the sluice water right out to the bar of sand, persistently formed where the Hayle river met the sea. Building this wall and the immense weir – both on sand – were feats of civil engineering in days when the excavation tool was the shovel and the transport was provided by the horse-drawn wagon and the mule.

The people of Hayle would have become accustomed to the sight and sound of the water when it was released from the Copperhouse Dock to scour the channel down to the harbour. Even so, they must have been excited and impressed nearly two hundred years ago when for the first time they saw and heard the water, let out from the Copperhouse Pool, cascade with great force through the shutters of the floodgates and flow rapidly down into the harbour and out to the bar.

Some time must have elapsed before the new sluicing arrangements scoured the waterways and harbour entrance sufficiently and no doubt the 'devil' was used from time to time to loosen the impacted sand to help flush it away. That the scheme was a great success is without question as larger ships began to use the port without difficulty. Further proof of this success came some years later when the Cornish Copper Company, as part of its anti-Harvey campaign, stopped sluicing for a time and the harbour soon began to silt up again.

In June 1983 as part of a flood prevention scheme for Hayle, the South West Water Authority replaced the old flood gates with new ones. These are designed to operate automatically so as to allow the Copperhouse Pool to fill up to a pre-determined level and release the water to flush the harbour waterways at low tide.

The Swing-Bridge

To get to and from the north and south sides of the harbour meant a tedious journey around the edges of the Est Loe. When the embankment was built to form it into the Copperhouse Pool all that was necessary to shorten the journey was a bridge over the floodgates. The first was a wooden one, moveable by some means, so that vessels could pass through the gates when open, and make their way to and from the Copperhouse Dock. The bridge was inadequate when, in 1832 the Cornish Copper Company, following the loss of its right to East Quay, had to make more use of North Quay. The company replaced the old bridge with a new cast iron one which was made in its foundry at Copperhouse. This bridge could be withdrawn when ships were due to pass into the channel to the Copperhouse quays. According to a report in the *West Briton* of 7 September 1832 the first loads over the bridge were eight wagons containing 28 tons of ore belonging to the Mines Royal Company. On the foremost wagon one of the company's agents took his station displaying an appropriate flag. Whether this was a ceremonial gesture, or served some purpose was not revealed. As the Hayle Railway line was to be routed over the floodgates something even more substantial was necessary to take the weight of the engines and wagons, as well as the horse-drawn traffic, so in 1837 another bridge was installed as a replacement by the Railway Company. This remained in operation until 1880 when it was replaced by a swing-bridge built by Harvey & Company for the Great Western Railway Company. In 1936 the Railway Company wanted to replace the swing-bridge, which was in need of repair, with a fixed one but there were legal difficulties. Although the use of the canal to Copperhouse had long since been discontinued for commercial shipping the public still retained the right of passage to and from the Pool. When the Railway Company found that it could not buy out this ancient right it had in mind to obtain powers to do so under an Act of Parliament. However, when the strength of the local opposition to these proposals was realised they were abandoned. About this time the owner of the MV *White Star* sought to exercise his right to take it through the floodgates into Copperhouse Pool and this could not be done without swinging the bridge on its old pivot. There were problems but, the Great Western Railway Company had to oblige, and only with difficulty was the bridge re-positioned.

Proposed Improvements

In 1801 the first attempt was made to carry out work in the port of Hayle under an Act of Parliament. In that year the Cornish Copper Company presented a

Petition to the House of Commons setting forth how it had expended considerable sums of money in erecting 'Flood Gates, making a Mound, Bank or Jettee near the Mouth of the River' for the convenience of shipping. It was desired to lengthen the 'Jettee' by about 5 feet to assist the clearance of sand and deepen the harbour 'for the Reception and safe lying of Ships, until they shall have Water, to the places of taking in or delivering their cargoes.' To cover the cost of the work it was intended to collect dues from ships entering the harbour. The Petitioners asked leave to bring in a Bill to carry out their proposals and on the Petition being heard by the House of Commons on 18 March 1801,(18) it was referred to a Committee with orders to examine it, call objectors and others, and report back to the House.

Unfortunately, in 1834 a fire at the House of Commons destroyed many records including those of the proceedings of the Committee ordered to deal with the Cornish Copper Company's Petition. Although the record of the decision of the Committee has been lost it must have been unfavourable for the Petitioners as no Act of Parliament ensued. At the meetings of the Committee the objectors to the proposals would have been heard and it is safe to assume that the strongest opposition came from the Harveys. They would have seen the proposals as an attempt by the Cornish Copper Company to get a statutory stranglehold and monopoly powers over the development of the port of Hayle and its operation.

The Steampacket Bridge

In about 1808 a channel was dug through the northern end of the embankment built to form the Copperhouse Pool. The channel was then bridged to carry the road to North Quay and fitted with sluice gates. According to the information handed down through the years not enough of the sluice water released through the 1788 floodgates found its way into the main waterway of the harbour. So the additional sluices were installed and by opening them at the same time as the others a strong flow of water was directed against the main stream to deflect it in the required direction.

The builders of the bridge over the channel could not have foreseen what loads it had to bear in the years ahead and it is a tribute to their workmanship that more than a century and a half passed before the bridge began to show signs of stress. In the 1960s under the great weights of heavily laden coal lorries, tankers from the oil depot on North Quay and Harvey's diesel cranes, cracks began to appear in the arch of the bridge and the road over it began to subside. The local authority had taken over the responsibility for the maintenance of the road some forty years before; but who owned the bridge? On the face of it Harvey & Company, as successors of the Cornish Copper Company, the builders, but the provisions of an old Act of Parliament, which provided for the transfer of old bridges of proven age into public ownership, cast doubt on this.

After protracted negotiations between the interested parties it was decided to discontinue using the old sluice gates and large diameter concrete pipes were embedded under the bridge. These were necessary so that the outflow of effluent from the Associated Octel factory into the harbour could continue. After the factory was closed in 1973 the channel was filled in.

In addition to the ancient quay at Lelant, later brought into use as the Lelant Brewery Quay already described, two other small quays were built and a dock was made, in the eighteenth century, on the western side of the Hayle harbour.

Norwayman's Dock

For the purpose of its merchanting business the Cornish Copper Company needed large quantities of foreign grown softwood which it imported from Norway.

Apart from being too large to sail far into the harbour the ships, heavily laden with timber, could not always be certain of reaching Hayle after a long voyage to catch the tides when they were at their highest. Some arrangement for berthing these ships as near as possible to deep water was necessary so in 1771 the company leased a plot of ground 200 feet by 60 feet near the edge of the river under Lelant 'to dig and maintain a dock'.(19) Time and tide have obliterated this dock which appropriately was called the Norwayman's Dock, but from old maps it would appear that it lay on the Lelant foreshore opposite the end of the weir running down the centre of the harbour. At the dock the berthed ships were unloaded over the sides and the large baulks of timber were floated down the harbour to timber ponds where they remained until needed. The smaller pieces were taken to the quays in lighters.

Griggs Quay

Until the Hayle Causeway was built in 1825 pedestrians and travellers on horses crossed from Hayle to the west over the sands at low tide, but wagons loaded with coal and other goods had to make the relatively long journey around via St Erth bridge. To shorten this the Cornish Copper Company, in 1775, rented a plot of ground in the tenement of Griggs at the western end of the Hayle estuary with the right 'to erect a quay or wharf for landing goods and to clean the channel of the river to preserve navigation'.(20) When this quay was built – to be known as Griggs Quay – small vessels could make their way directly to it and goods were also sent over by lighter en route to the west. In due course Henry Harvey took over this quay and used it, even after the Hayle Causeway was built, so as to avoid the tolls demanded for its use.

Ordnance Quay

The other quay which lay on the western side of the harbour was a small one which was later incorporated in a new quay built by the Praeds of Trevethoe in the 1870s. It was known at one time as Newton's Quay and later as the Ordnance Quay.(21)

When the West Cornwall Railway sought Parliamentary approval in 1847 to purchase and extend the East Quay it also petitioned for powers to lay a railway line to the Ordnance Quay which would have needed the building of an embankment to carry it across the estuary. Admiralty objections to such an arrangement were upheld and the scheme was abandoned. In the previous year the Cornwall & Devon Central Railway had applied unsuccessfully for permission to lay a line from St Erth to the Ordnance Quay.

Penpol Channel

In the year 1779, John Harvey, the enterprising blacksmith of Carnhell in the nearby parish of Gwinear appeared on the scene and built an iron foundry on land he had leased at Carnsew on the southern edge of the harbour. In the following year he secured the right from Lord Arundell, who owned much of the Penpol estate, to dig a channel to his foundry from deep water so that vessels could come up to it and discharge their cargoes of coal and pig-iron alongside instead of lying aground in the harbour to be unloaded there.(22)

The channel was to be made by widening and deepening the Penpol stream which divided the estates of Penpol and Carnsew. For years after 1793, when a start was made to dig the channel, attempts to complete it were frustrated by the Cornish Copper Company which sent men to dump slag and rubbish in the excavations claiming, on one pretext or another, that damage was being caused to the crossing place from the Royal Standard Inn across the sands to Lelant and Penzance. This was a patch of hard sand athwart the Penpol stream, but John Harvey had no intention to cut through it in making his channel. The Cornish Copper Company also claimed that it had acquired (in 1788) Lord

Arundell's interests in Penpol and the conveyance did not expressly exclude the right he had granted to John Harvey to dig a channel on the property. It was not that the partners of the Cornish Copper Company were against the channel as such, and they even declared that they would give the Harveys every assistance if their activities were confined to iron founding. What caused them to act as they did was their knowledge of Harvey's ambition to branch out as a merchant to supply coal and other seaborne goods to the local mines. This business was profitable and the Cornish Copper Company, by various means, had gained the monopoly of it and it was very determined to hold on to it by fair means or foul.

The battles that accompanied the attempts of the Harveys to dig their channel to the foundry along the bed of the Penpol stream were fought on and off for many years and it was not until 1818 that the final attempt was made to complete the task. A start was made by putting twenty men to work, but after three weeks the Cornish Copper Company made it known that it intended to fill in the excavations so far made. Thus warned, Henry Harvey trebled the number of diggers and when one morning, a large party from Copperhouse arrived on the scene and started to fill in the channel, Harvey's men threw the sand and mud out again. This performance went on for the whole day 'to the great terror of the neighbourhood'. The struggle was resumed the next morning when Henry Harvey doubled the number of his diggers and completely foiled his opponents by loading the mud and sand directly into carts which were immediately driven away. Thus thwarted, the Cornish Copper Company abandoned the struggle and the channel was completed in a further five weeks. Ships of 150 tons burden could then sail right up to the foundry.

Looking back on these extraordinary events from the safe distance of time they take on the appearance of a farce, but for the adversaries the 'digging out' by one side and the 'filling in' by the other was a battle for supremacy and a very serious matter. The old antagonism of their masters – which continued for long after – was reflected in the enmity between the men of Copperhouse and Foundry. During the frenzied shovelling in the mud much hand-to-hand fighting took place we are told and no doubt those on both sides made the most of their chances to settle old scores.

Foundry Quay

During the long years of conflict the ambition of the Harveys to expand their business was restricted because although the completion of the Penpol channel had improved their prospects they lacked their own quay on which to store coal and also copper ore which they could offer to ship to South Wales as return cargoes. The parcels of ore which could be extracted from the mines had to be stored separately when they awaited shipment and this arrangement took up much space.

In 1817 Henry Harvey had become the tenant of that part of the Carnsew estate which included the wastrel as the landlords had favoured him with a new lease instead of the Cornish Copper Company whose tenancy had expired. As a result he was in a position to build his long wanted quay and he set about it immediately after completing the Penpol channel in the following year. This quay to be called Foundry Quay, and sometimes South Quay, was constructed on the western bank of the channel. Whatever bedrock was there was too deep to be used for the quay's foundations and the courses of the quay wall, consisting of massive blocks of granite, were placed on layers of furze faggots which served as a base. As the wall was built up it was filled in behind with sand and mud. To allow surface water to drain away the walls were not pointed with mortar. As a result quantities of infill were always being washed out and the receding tidal water added to the erosion. In consequence, the surface of the quay had to be topped up to its original level from time to time.

It is to be wondered at how a quay built on such insubstantial foundations could stand for long, but it was not until some one hundred and fifty years later, in the early 1970s, that a section of the quay wall collapsed through decay.

A feature of Foundry Quay is that it is not in a straight line and the eastern wall has a series of curvatures in its length. It is believed that the purpose of this design was to enable sailing ships to berth with their bowsprits canting outwards so that they could tie up close to each other. One of the main reasons for building this quay was to store copper ore awaiting shipment. It is likely that the overall length of the vessels would have exceeded the width of the individual ore plots – each walled off from its neighbour, but by overlapping, the ships could still lie near the plot from which they were to be loaded.

The cost of building Foundry Quay was £9,000, a very large amount in 1818. It was more than Henry Harvey could find from his own resources and he was assisted by his bankers Daniell & Willyams of Truro who lent him a substantial sum. Now in opposition to the Cornish Copper Company, Henry Harvey lost no time in seeking to raise revenue from his new quay and was soon canvassing the Welsh smelters with offers to ship out their copper ore from it.

As might be expected, Foundry Quay was not built without incident. As its construction proceeded the partners of the Cornish Copper Company were surprised at the size of it, and concerned about the effect on their business if it was completed and brought into use. By threatening legal proceedings they attempted to halt further work on the quay, but to no avail, and Henry Harvey pressed on and built his quay northwards as far as the ford across the Penpol stream opposite the Royal Standard inn.

East Quay

Unable to prevent the completion of the Foundry Quay by legal means the Cornish Copper Company, as determined and vengeful as ever in its opposition to the Harveys, decided that the proposed extension of Foundry Quay beyond the ford could be rendered useless for shipping by building a wall or quay so close to it that the passage to it would be obstructed.

By this time Henry Harvey had acquired a two-thirds leasehold interest in the Carnsew estate and had taken the precaution of marking its boundary with the Penpol estate by setting up stone markers. According to Harvey's determination the dividing line lay along the old bed of the Penpol river and not the one then existing, which he contended was made further to the west of the original bed by the action of the sluice water from the Copperhouse Pool. The confirmation of the line of the boundary between Carnsew and Penpol became the subject of an important legal case a few years later.

If the quay proposed by the Cornish Copper Company was to serve its purpose as an obstruction to the use of Foundry Quay then a part of it had to be built on the Carnsew estate which would take it over the border line marked by Henry Harvey. The other part would lie in Penpol on land already owned by the Cornish Copper Company.

The company's first move was to get rid of the tell-tale boundary stones and under cover of darkness and when all was quiet on the night of Sunday 16 November 1818, a party of about forty men was assembled to do this. It so happened that they were seen by a Harvey employee who hastened to Henry to tell him that something was afoot. Sensing trouble once again, he got together a similar number of his workmen and set out to confront his opponents. Inevitably, there was a skirmish, but by midnight both sides had had enough for one day. After a night's rest the 'battle' was resumed, but by now each side had mustered hundreds of men. Anticipating this crowd and a new outbreak of violence, Henry Harvey had that morning summoned the nearest magistrate, the Rev Samuel Stephens, the vicar of St Erth, in the hope that he could use his authority to prevent further conflict. He duly arrived on the scene – but not before Henry Harvey had been knocked down earlier in the melee – and was able to bring about the disengagement of the two parties. Not only that, he persuaded them to agree in writing that either should be at liberty to complete their quays on the opposite banks of the Penpol river without molestation from the other.

With this notable truce arranged and left in peace at last, Henry Harvey set about lengthening his Foundry Quay by a further one hundred yards from the ford across the Penpol stream and over which he built an archway. This was filled in sometime after the Hayle Causeway was made in 1825. It must have remained a weak point in the quay as there was a collapse there in the 1960s probably caused by the weight of scrap metal then stored on it.

For their part the partners of the Cornish Copper Company continued with their own quay to be known as East Quay and for a time as John Oliver's Quay from the name of a merchant who traded from it and lived in the cottage on the quay. Restricted in their building, by the agreement with Henry Harvey, to the eastern bank of the Penpol river, the extremity of the company's new quay came nowhere near obstructing access to Foundry Quay and was separated some forty yards from it. This outcome must have been foreseen before work started on East Quay and its continuance must have been a face-saving operation. Not only was the quay to be a failure as an obstruction to Henry Harvey as intended, but the Cornish Copper Company already had sufficient quay space at North Quay and elsewhere. At £5,000, the building of East Quay at 1820 prices, was therefore a costly exercise and the time was not far distant when the company would lose most of it.

In 1827 Henry Harvey became the sole leaseholder of the Carnsew estate and was in a position to turn the tables on his old rivals. He had long maintained that the old course of the Penpol river forming the boundary between Carnsew and Penpol had been pushed westward by the action of sluicing from the Copperhouse Pool. It will be remembered that he set up stones to mark what he considered to be the boundary line in earlier days. In the agreement made in 1818 between him and the Cornish Copper Company, which allowed each side to proceed with the building of their quays, this contention of Henry Harvey as to the old boundary was not taken into account. However, he now revived his claim and persuaded his landlords to take action to recover the piece of Carnsew land between the old and new beds of the Penpol river. If the claim was upheld then that part of East Quay built on it would also fall into their hands. After a legal battle which lasted, on and off, for five years the claim of the Carnsew landlords was upheld and they – and in turn Henry Harvey – secured the absolute rights over a large part of East Quay including access to it. It was a condition of the settlement that the Cornish Copper Company was to be offered the quay on a tenancy agreement, but this was declined in spite of the fact that the part of the quay which remained in its possession was virtually useless for shipping.

Triumphant, Henry Harvey made good use of his part of East Quay on which he constructed fourteen copper ore plots, most of which he leased to copper smelters such as the English Copper Company and the Mines Royal Company, to store ore bought by them and to be shipped to South Wales for smelting. This ore came down from the Camborne and Redruth mines on the Hayle Railway's line in trucks which were run onto a siding alongside the plots into which the ore was conveniently unloaded.

In 1846 the West Cornwall Railway petitioned the House of Commons to be allowed to extend its line between Hayle and Redruth, eastward to Truro and westward to Penzance. Parliament agreed and the enabling Act was passed, but inserted in it was a clause requiring the Railway Company to apply for powers to provide a public wharf at Hayle.(23) This was done by a Petition dated 29 January 1847 for leave to bring in a Bill 'to build a new quay or wharf, 2,000 feet long for landing passengers and goods on the eastern side of the estuary'.(24) From the plan which accompanied the petition it can be seen that the new quay was to be a southward extension of East Quay, facing Penpol Terrace and parallel to Foundry Quay. As a preliminary, the Railway Company agreed to buy East Quay from Henry Harvey for £11,500. Nothing came of this proposal to build a new quay as Parliament, having instigated it, then threw it out, on the grounds that no railway company ought to become a trading company!

It is of interest that, in the documents submitted to Parliament, East Quay was shown as Lawyers Wharf, a name not found elsewhere. The reason for this name is not hard to find. A couple of decades previously the legal fraternity had fought on and off for five years to establish the ownership of this quay and it was, therefore, aptly named.

The permanent walled enclosures or plots on East Quay in which copper ore was stored were built on the western edge of it at which ships could tie up. So the quay could be used for little else, but when copper mining ceased the ore shipments were replaced by a variety of cargoes. Coal came in for the Hayle Gasworks erected nearby in 1889, and a few years later Hosken, Trevithick, Polkinhorn & Company Ltd, millers of Loggans, used the quay for its grain imports and also rented space to handle general cargoes carried by its steamer *M.J.Hedley*. Between the wars this service was operated by Gilchrist & Company, Coast Lines Ltd and J. Bibby & Sons Ltd until the 1950s. Cargoes of potatoes and fertilisers found their way inland via East Quay and from it explosives were shipped by ICI Ltd until it purchased Lelant Quay for the purpose in 1948.

Bristolman's Dock

Another small quay which was an early feature of the port was the Bristolman's Dock which lay just outside the Copperhouse Pool floodgates. As its name implies, it was used by vessels on the Hayle/Bristol run which began towards the end of the eighteenth century.

The Basin or Carnsew Pool

The penultimate structural addition to the port of Hayle took a different form to those that had been made before. The Carnsew landlords' action against the Cornish Copper Company to recover that part of the estate on which a section of the new East Quay was built came to trial in 1829 but the various legal processes leading up to it started well before that. When the company learned of the intentions to attempt to dispossess it of a part of its quay it retaliated by ceasing to sluice regularly and operated the gates only when it was necessary for its own purposes. In consequence the waterway to Foundry Quay soon began to silt up as the Cornish Copper Company intended that it should. It then attempted to get Henry Harvey to agree to make an annual payment in return for the resumption of regular sluicing, but not being one to yield under duress, and probably doubting the Cornish Copper Company's good faith from previous experience, he would have none of it. He also had in mind a scheme which, if he could carry it out, would solve his sluicing problems once and for all.

Henry Harvey's idea was to build at Carnsew, on part of the south-western arm of the estuary a tidal reservoir, complete with floodgates, so that he could impound the water on the incoming tide and release it after the ebb and thus to scour out the channel to his Foundry and East Quays.

To carry out these proposals, at the time they were considered, was a major civil engineering undertaking with a requirement for extensive excavations, a mile of embankment of massive proportions and large floodgates similar to those at the entrance to Copperhouse Pool. There was doubt as to whether a project of this magnitude was within the planning and constructional capabilities of anyone locally so the engagement of the services of the celebrated civil engineer, Thomas Telford of road building fame, was considered. However, Henry Harvey went ahead on his own and started to build his reservoir in 1833 and completed it in the December of the following year. In its time it has been given a number of names – 'the Basin', 'the Forty Acres', and the 'Carnsew Pool'. To mark the successful completion of his project Henry Harvey invited a large number of his friends to breakfast and to witness the first sluicing of the channel on 27 December 1834. Not neglected in these celebrations were the men employed on the work, sixty of whom were given dinner at the White Hart Inn then kept by Henry's sister, Mrs Trevithick. An entry, dated 5 January 1835, in the Harvey Cash Book records that the meals for the men were 3/- each. At that time, and at that price, the fare – no doubt well washed down with liquor – must have been substantial, and even more so for the four foremen or captains as they were called, entertained at 4/- each.

In addition to the anxieties Henry Harvey must have had during the planning and construction of his enormous pool there was also the problem of paying for it. The profits from the thriving foundry were used to finance its expansion so there was little available immediately from that source. However, he privately owned some valuable leasehold property which he mortgaged for a loan of £7,200 at 4½% interest from Sir Charles Lemon. The number of vessels using the Harvey quays increased following the success of the new sluicing arrangements, but the dues levied on them were insufficient to meet the interest charges and pay off the loan. Nevertheless, from his business as a whole Henry Harvey was able to discharge his debt by 1838.

A hundred years after the Basin was completed there came a new use for the water impounded in it which Henry Harvey could not have foreseen. By 1938 the output from the Hayle Electric Power Station had increased to such an extent that an additional and constant supply of water was required for cooling purposes. A proposal to draw this from the Copperhouse Pool was abandoned as was a scheme to dam the water in the Lelant estuary to form a reservoir. In 1939 came another plan, which was carried out. The Basin, below the level of its floodgates was deepened so that all the water did not flow out when the harbour was sluiced. From the water that remained a supply was pumped to the Power Station through a tunnel which was driven under the bed of the harbour.

Lelant Quay

No doubt moved to action by seeing the large number of ships using the quays on the eastern side of the port, the Praed family of Trevethoe, who owned the foreshore on the western side applied to the Board of Trade to build a new quay at Lelant. It was intended that it would be connected with the proposed branch railway line from St Erth to St Ives. Early in November 1871 the Board of Trade turned down the Praed's application, but changed its mind the following week and authorised the erection of the new quay. Doubtless, some intensive last minute lobbying of influential members of Parliament connected with the Board of Trade brought about this decision.

A start was made on building the quay which is 550 feet long and incorporates the old Ordnance Quay. It was completed at a cost of £16,000. It was a 'white elephant' from the start in spite of its advantages of a railway line and deep water berths. Shipments to and from the quay were confined to a few general cargoes from Bristol, coal for a Lelant merchant and pit-props from the Trevethoe estate.

In 1877 the owners of Lelant Quay applied to the Board of Trade for authority to levy dues on the users of it and to make bye-laws applicable to its use. Objections to the application were raised by Harvey & Company on the grounds that it did not include a provision to make a contribution towards maintaining the buoys and lights and sluicing the main harbour channel without which the use of the quay would be impossible. The Board of Trade suggested that the parties should get together to settle their differences but the outcome was the withdrawal of the application by the Praeds who were possibly discouraged because the quay had been little used since it was built.

Though the existence of the Lelant Quay proved to be of little importance the threat remained that this could change and in 1878, to ward off possible competitors, Harvey & Company leased the quay for nine years, but at the end of the term the lease was not renewed.

Over the years Lelant remained moribund and when in 1920 much of the Trevethoe estate was sold off, it was bought by Thos. W. Ward Ltd, of Sheffield. This company bought and scrapped many of the warships of the Royal Navy which were redundant after the end of the Great War. A number of the smaller ones were brought to the Lelant and Foundry Quays and broken up.

In 1948 Thos. W. Ward Ltd sold Lelant Quay to ICI Ltd, this company needing an isolated wharf from which it could ship explosives from its factory (formerly Bickford-Smith's) at Tuckingmill, Camborne. The company, at considerable expense, improved the storage facilities, but the berth at Lelant, which was bypassed by the main sluicing channel, was often 'foul' and unfit for vessels to lie on. The technical resources of ICI were brought to bear in an attempt to overcome this problem and an expensive artificial berth of stones encaged in a metal grid was laid down. Even this was not wholly successful as ridges of sand formed on it, and they had to be cleared away by the time-honoured method of shovelling.

When ICI Ltd closed its Tuckingmill factory Lelant Quay was put up for sale and it was bought in 1962 by Harvey & Company, not with the immediate intention of using it for its seaborne trade, but to exclude competition, the purpose for which it had leased the quay a hundred years before. For a time it was used by the Union Corporation as a base for tin recovery operations using sand dredged from St Ives Bay. Then once again, in the 1970s Lelant Quay was used for shipbreaking, but this time old Fleetwood trawlers were scrapped there.

There was great consternation in July 1982 when a very large deposit of blue asbestos was revealed by the action of high tides near Lelant Quay. When it was buried, the danger to health through exposure to asbestos dust was not then realised and the removal of the deposit had to be undertaken with great care. It is possible that the asbestos came from the cladding of the boilers and pipework of ships broken up at Lelant in the 1920s.

Communications

TO PROGRESS IN its growth a port needs a good road system through the surrounding countryside, something which the port of Hayle did not have in the early years of its development. In the eighteenth century the condition of the Cornish roads was atrocious. Little more than tracks, they were rutted and uneven, awash in the winter and they crumbled in the summer. Coal imported into Hayle and destined for the mines and return loads of copper ore were carried on the backs of horses and mules. We are told that as many as '500 and sometimes up to 1,000' animals could, in the mid-eighteenth century, be seen daily carrying coal from Hayle to the mines.(25) Later on, four-wheeled wagons were used, but pulling them fully laden and trying to prevent them from overturning on the rough tracks was hard on man and beast.

For centuries the upkeep of the so-called roads was a parish responsibility, and there was little enthusiasm to spend money to keep them in good repair for through traffic. A turnpike road, financed by public subscription and maintained from the receipt of tolls, was made between Truro and Redruth in 1754, and between Falmouth and Marazion in 1761, but elsewhere in West Cornwall the state of the roads remained unchanged. Nothing came of proposals in 1799 to build a turnpike road between Redruth and Ludgvan which would have necessitated a bridge or causeway between Hayle and Griggs across the sands of the estuary which were impassable except at low water, and this inconvenience for travellers to and from the west was not overcome until 1825 when a causeway was built across the estuary under the authority of the Hayle Turnpike Act. In its preamble great stress was laid on the importance and extensive trade of the port of Hayle. By 1838 the route from the end of the causeway to Penzance had been turnpiked, followed in 1840, by that from Hayle to Redruth.(26) This road bypassed Angarrack and the notoriously steep Steamers Hill into and out of the village.

Although these improvements made to the roads between the towns went some way towards easing the problems of traffic to and from Hayle, the mines to which most of it went and returned, were well off the beaten track and once the turnpikes were left behind conditions were as bad as ever. The Highways Act of 1835 encouraged parishes to combine to maintain their roads and with the further local government developments which followed the condition of the by-ways was gradually improved.

The eighteenth century was the age of canal building in England. The circumstances which gave rise to the construction of these waterways to provide a cheap and efficient means of transport between the industrial centres of the Midlands and the coal fields and the ports did not apply to any extent in Cornwall as the very hilly nature of the county made it difficult to build canals. Nevertheless, in 1796 there was a proposal to construct a canal from Hayle to Gweek via St Erth, Nancegollan and Helston passing through one of the busiest mining districts.(27) Surveys were carried out and cost and profit calculations were made, but the project was abandoned, as was another scheme in 1801, for a canal from Hayle to Camborne via Angarrack and a tram line to Helston in 1819.(28)

The year 1831 marked a great improvement in travel arrangements by sea with the introduction of a regular steampacket service between Hayle and Bristol for passengers and small consignments of goods of various kinds. The first of these packets was the *Herald* and later, at intervals came the *Cornwall*, *Brilliant*, *Express*, *Queen*, *Bride*, *Albion* and *Bessie*.

The Cornish Copper Company had an interest in the *Brilliant*, *Queen* and *Albion* packets which docked at the company's North Quay on which there had been an inn as early as 1779.(29) This was the Britannia, renamed the Steampacket Hotel in 1842 when it was refurbished to provide refreshment and overnight accommodation for the passengers of the *Brilliant* which came on station in that year. The White Hart, in Foundry Square served those travellers using the Harvey packets, the *Herald*, *Cornubia* and others. For those who wished to use it there was also the Royal Standard Inn mid-way between the other two.

On land a stagecoach service which could be used by the packet ships' passengers to and from Hayle was started and by 1839 the *Defiance* and the *Regulator* were running between Hayle and Truro calling at the White Hart in the mornings and afternoons.(30) In this year the White Hart was enlarged and the proprietor, William Crotch, with an eye to the extra business it would produce for his new establishment, set up his own omnibus service between Hayle and Penzance as an additional convenience for the steampacket passengers.(31)

Among the illustrations is one of a painting c1843 of the *Brilliant* stagecoach passing Ponsandane House, Penzance on its way to Hayle. The coach carried on its side the notice 'From Penzance to the Hayle Railway and Steamer' but it is unlikely that it was Crotch's vehicle. Its name 'Brilliant' suggests that it served the steampacket of that name, introduced in 1842 by the Cornish Copper Company, the arch-rival of Henry Harvey, Crotch's shipowning landlord.

In 1837 there came a new method of communication with Hayle as, in that year, the Hayle Railway Company completed the laying of its line between the port and Tresavean in the parish of Gwennap. Its initial purpose was to carry copper ore and coal between Hayle and the mines in the Camborne and Redruth district, but arrangements were made later to carry passengers. The effect this new method of transport had on the old one, using horse-drawn wagons, can be gauged by the tonnages handled by the railway and which were taken off the indifferent roads. In the years from 1843 to 1846 well over 62,000 tons of copper ore were shipped from the Harvey quays and more than three-quarters of the total reached Hayle by rail from the Camborne and Redruth mines.(32) Large tonnages of ore were also railed to Hayle for shipment by the Cornish Copper Company. In addition many train loads of coal were sent up to the mines from the quays.

The Hayle Railway Company introduced its passenger service between Hayle and Redruth in 1841 and this provided a more convenient method of travel between the towns than the stagecoaches which could carry only a few passengers at a time. This same year saw the opening of the rail link between Bristol and London and it became possible to travel from West Cornwall by one of the packet vessels from Hayle to Bristol and then on to London, in far less time than it took all the way by stagecoach, the only other means available – apart from horseback and by sea – before 1841.

In favourable conditions the early packet steamers took about fourteen hours to make passage from Hayle to Bristol and this time was reduced as faster vessels came on station later. The rail journey from Bristol to London took four and a half hours so, under favourable conditions, the traveller from Hayle to London could get there in a day.

The popularity of the Hayle/Bristol steampacket service is evidenced by the tally of passengers travelling between the ports in 1845. In that year the number taking passage in the *Herald* and *Cornwall* was 7,593.(33)

Communications between Hayle and other parts of Cornwall were further improved in 1852 when the Hayle/Redruth line was extended westwards to Penzance and eastwards to Truro. Then in 1859, with the completion of Brunel's bridge over the Tamar, came the railway link between Cornwall and London. By this time the stagecoaches had had their day and the steampackets from Hayle began to face the competition of rail travel and finally succumbed to it when the last of them, the *Bride*, was withdrawn from service in 1874.

With the establishment of the railway network, branch lines to the Hayle quays were essential and the first was laid by the Hayle Railway Company to North Quay and another followed to East Quay. A remnant of the old Hayle Railway became the branch to Foundry Quay and as the old track was unsuitable for an engine, horses were used for more than a hundred years to haul trucks along the line. The unique sight of these horses at work disappeared in 1961 when they were replaced by a motor tractor.

The use of the line from Hayle railway station to North Quay continued until 1981 when the Esso fuel oil depot, to which supplies were railed after shipments ceased, closed down in February of that year.

Methods of Cargo Handling

THE METHODS OF discharging cargoes in the port of Hayle in the early days of its development were primitive. The main import was coal which was shovelled into baskets as it lay in the ship's hold and in these it was slung on to the quay if the vessel was able to get alongside it. When low tides prevented this and the vessel had to lie aground in the harbour and the coal was heaved into panniers which were slung across the backs of mules and horses and carried away.

Mechanical means of discharging cargoes of coal made their appearance in 1829 for the first time with an invention of Richard Trevithick. The loaded baskets of coal were hoisted from the ship's hold and swung ashore by means of a small portable steam engine which could be set up on board ship. The baskets when emptied were automatically returned to the hold for re-loading. Like many of the Trevithick inventions this one was before its time and attempts to market it for use at other ports were unsuccessful.

A report in the *Cornish Telegraph* of 17 August 1870 describes an accident in which William Richards, the mate of the *Bessie* was killed. To discharge the 370 tons of coal the vessel carried, a stage was erected over the hold, secured by tackle at each corner. The men worked from this when digging out the cargo. On this occasion one corner of the stage gave away and fell on to Richards who was leaning on the bulwarks.

In the 1890s mobile steam cranes were introduced. At this time some 100,000 tons of coal were being imported annually. With the new cranes, which had a lift of 30 cwts., a cargo of 620 tons could be unloaded in a day and a half by two of them and twenty-eight men, most of whom shovelled the coal into steel tubs which were then hoisted ashore. These steam cranes were simple in operation, reliable and economical in use. The main cost of keeping them in working order was a new boiler from time to time.

In addition to their use at the various quays in the port the steam cranes were also employed in discharging coal for the Electric Power Station at its berth at North Quay. By 1938 its consumption of coal had increased to such an extent that some quicker means of unloading the cargoes became necessary. The authorities then installed a battery of electric cranes to deal exclusively at any time with the procession of ships coming in.

In the 1950s the steam cranes then in use came to the end of their useful life and were replaced by modern diesel models with a much greater lifting capacity of 5 tons and the ability to grab out coal from ships' holds. In the course of a working day two of the new cranes could discharge a cargo of 800 tons with ten men.

Harvey & Company was among the first port owners to unload cargoes of bagged cement by means of pallets. Thirty bags were placed onto a wooden platform – the pallet – which was then swung ashore either onto a forklift truck and taken into the store, or onto a customer's lorry. By this method introduced in the 1950s, 400 tons of bagged cement could be unloaded from a vessel in a day.

Up to the time when coal cargoes were discharged from the ships by a grab attachment to the diesel cranes, large numbers of quay porters or dockers, to give them their modern name, were employed to fill the tubs in the ships' holds, for hoisting ashore. These men were employed on a casual basis until 1943, and mustered in the mornings and afternoons hoping to be selected for any work on hand. If there was insufficient for all of them those not required went away unpaid. Rarely was there a sufficient number of ships in the port at any one time to ensure employment for all the dockers and as opportunities for work of another kind were few there was hardship among them. To overcome this problem the National Dock Labour Scheme was introduced in 1943 and under this each port had a permanent gang of dockers allotted to it. They continued to report for work as before, but if not employed, were paid an attendance allowance financed by a levy on the port employers. If there was insufficient work for them at their home port the dockers could be taken to other ports in the district where extra labour was required.

In the early days of its importation into Hayle much of the timber came in as large baulks. The ships carrying them berthed at the Norwayman's Dock near the entrance to the harbour. The baulks were off-loaded, made up into rafts and towed to a timber pond – Harvey's at Carnsew and the Cornish Copper Company's in the Copperhouse Pool. From these ponds the baulks were taken from time to time and cut up in the sawmills.

In the course of time, most of the timber imported into Hayle was sawn into various lengths and sizes, beforehand, by the shippers. Unloading timber in this form was as laborious as in baulk, as the pieces – and there were thousands of them in an average cargo – had to be made up into bundles to be swung ashore, either by crane, or the ship's derricks. By the latest method timber is made up before shipment, by length and size, into packs ready for discharging. Not long after this innovation, in the 1960s, timber imports into the port of Hayle ceased.

Scrap iron was an export from Hayle from the early 1920s when Thos. W. Ward Ltd began breaking up old warships. Awkward stuff to handle it was usually dropped straight into the ship's hold. In the 1950s when industrial and domestic scrap iron was exported from Hayle the diesel cranes were fitted with spider grabs when loading ships. These grabs were a great advance and with their steel arms, spider-like in shape, and their ability to enfold and lift the scrap, they were well named.

Navigation – Lights and Pilots

FROM THE SEAWARD side the entrance to Hayle Harbour at the south-west corner of St Ives Bay is not easy to pick out at sea level against the background of the Hayle and Lelant Towans. This problem with the hazard of the sand bar at the mouth of the harbour and the shifting channels within, made conditions for a passage to the port difficult in the best of weather, particularly for sailing vessels with their limited ability to manoeuvre.

To keep the entrance channel to the harbour straight the Cornish Copper Company made an embankment along its western side and on it placed guiding posts. The eastern side was marked by a series of buoys later reduced to two to indicate the bar.

For navigation at night time lights for guidance were essential. The earliest lights were probably provided by the occupants of Carnsew Fort which lies in a direct line with the harbour entrance.[34] Later in medieval times, it is thought that a guiding light was shown in the tiny chapel that once stood on the Anja or Anta Rock at the mouth of the harbour and now almost buried in the sand.[35] The lighting for guidance in more modern times dates from about 1838 when two fixed lights 92 yards apart and visible from the sea at six miles in clear weather were erected on the Lelant bank of the entrance channel. The lights were lit at night when there was a depth of water of 12 feet or more over the bar.[36] They were so placed that when lined up by an approaching vessel it was led directly to the bar. Lights were also placed at the end of the weir to mark the point at which the channel in the harbour divided. The guiding lights were lit by electricity in 1916.

In the 1950s a signalling system was installed at the Ferry to indicate the depth of water over the bar during the hours of daylight. It consisted of a tide gauge calibrated to give the bar depths and a signal consisting of two arms which could be raised to indicate to an incoming vessel when sufficient water was available to cross the bar safely. When a number of ships were due to enter or leave the harbour on a tide the signals were also used to control their passage through the narrow entrance channel.

After the Electric Power Station was enlarged in 1950 it required so much more coal that a shuttle service operating day and night had to be arranged to bring it from South Wales. This meant the 24-hour movement of vessels in and out of the port when the tides were favourable and to improve the facilities for navigation at night more lights were erected and were placed along the western bank of the entrance channel; at Chapel Anja Rock; on the North Quay and the weir.

Local and up-to-date knowledge of the course of the harbour waterways and their depth has always been essential to ensure a safe passage in and out of the port. Before the establishment of the Trinity House Pilotage Service following the Pilotage Act of 1838 ships were guided by local seamen, mainly from St Ives, acting as freelance pilots and known as 'hobblers'. They were able to charge what they liked for their services, and many masters refused to hire them on this account, sometimes with dire consequences.

When pilots licensed by Trinity House were appointed their employment by masters of vessels using the port was made compulsory by that authority.

Whereas steam vessels could make their way in and out of the harbour under their own power it was not so simple for sailing ships. They had to be warped in and out by boatmen making use of the posts placed to mark the western edge of the channel inwards from the bar. When the steampacket *Herald* came on station in 1831 and was in the harbour, she would, if the wind was unfavourable for sailing ships, tow them in and out for a moderate charge and save them from the tedious and time consuming exercise of warping.(37) From the 1860s they were assisted by the tug *Warrior* stationed at Hayle for this purpose. Afterwards, from 1890 - 1902 came the *North Star*.

In spite of the skill of the pilots ships, on occasion, ran aground when entering or leaving the port because of a sudden and unseen build-up of sand or a change in the course of the waterways. When groundings occurred which blocked the port's channels the consequences could be serious. One such event was the grounding of the fully laden tanker *Bridgman* in the harbour in the 1960s.

The size of the vessels able to use the port of Hayle was governed by their draughts when loaded and the depths of water over the bar and at the quays, which varied with the spring and neap tides. Before 1788, when the Cornish Copper Company impounded the water in the Est Loe to sluice and deepen the waterways, small vessels of some 80 to 100 tons burden could use the port, but then only at the height of the spring tides.(38) Conditions were further improved by the additional sluicing power provided by the Basin constructed in 1834.

The Channel Pilot of 1874, issued by the Admiralty, gave a height of water on the bar of 19 feet at High Water Springs and 13 feet at High Water Neaps which enabled vessels of 400 tons to get in and out. In 1903 it was reported that ships of up to 900 tons burden could use the port at maximum high water when there was from 17 to 20 feet of water at the various quays. The depths of water available on the bar and at the quays varied little over the years due to the efficiency of the sluicing arrangements. In the course of time steamers gave way to diesel-engined vessels of shallower draught and on spring tides ships up to 210 feet long and drawing 14½ feet of water and carrying up to 1000 tons could use the port.(39)

Tide Tables

As a knowledge of tide times was essential for shipowners tide tables for Hayle for issue to them were compiled annually. Initially, they were based on the tide levels at the Old Dock Sill at Liverpool, and later on, the high water depths at Cobh in Eire. The tables thus produced on this information proved sufficiently accurate for the port's shipping. However, in 1952 when a naval vessel HMS *Wave* went ashore in the Bay their precision was called into question by the Queen's Harbourmaster at Plymouth as lifting vessels, brought down to release HMS *Wave*, also remained aground when they should have floated according to the depth of water indicated by the tide tables! Future tables were then based on the predictions of the Liverpool Observatory and Tidal Institute.

Godrevy Lighthouse

An underwater hazard which faces ships making their way to and from Hayle and anywhere else in St Ives Bay, is a long reef of rocks on its eastern edge and known as the Stones. Swept on to them by gales and strong tides, scores of sailing ships met their end on these rocks, often with loss of life. In fog, or through errors in navigation steamships fared no better. One of these, the *Nile*, a new 700 tonner bound for Penzance from Liverpool and somehow off course, ploughed into the Stones on a November night in 1854 with the loss of all on board.

The magnitude of the disaster which befell the *Nile* revived the clamour of shipowners and others for a light to warn mariners of the presence of the Stones. This time action was taken by Trinity House which resulted in the erection of the Godrevy Lighthouse, but not until 1859 was it in operation, and not before the Stones had claimed other victims.

Rotten Row

During the winter months many fishing boats and other small craft were laid up at Hayle and made ready for sea in the spring and the place for this was on the foreshore facing Penpol Terrace. Here, large baulks of timber were placed on which the boats could rest and be worked on. This became known locally as Rotten Row(40) which suggests that many of them ended their days there in no condition to set sail again.

The Ferryman

This chapter would not be complete without a reference to the ferryman who once plied between the banks on either side of the harbour entrance. The ferry was used for centuries as the quickest way for travellers between Phillack and Lelant when the tide covered the sands of the harbour. The alternative was a long and uncomfortable detour via St Erth.

The ferry rights were owned by the Trevethoe estate until bought by Harvey & Company in 1921.

From his vantage point at the ferry the ferryman was well placed to see approaching vessels and hail them with warnings and advise of conditions and in the days of sail assist in warping them into harbour. When the daytime system of signalling a sufficient depth of water over the bar was introduced it was the ferryman's duty to hoist the indicator flag when necessary. It was also his job to light and maintain the oil navigation lights which were set up in 1838 to guide night-time arrivals.

The earliest known ferryman of whom there is a record was John Russell who died in 1832 aged 76. He was assisted at the ferry in his declining years by his daughter. The last ferryman was the legendary Jack Couch, a rare character with a seagoing background and a colourful vocabulary to match it which he delighted in using in his stentorian tones regardless of the company. He died in about 1966.

HM Customs and Port of Registry

THE CUSTOMS SERVICE in England and Wales is of great antiquity and dates from the early thirteenth century. It was established for the assessment and collection of duties levied on seaborne merchandise and to prevent the evasion of their payment by smuggling.

The Customs organisation, in its present form, dates from the setting-up of the Board of Customs in 1671. Certain ports were selected and declared as Customs Ports with a Collector in charge. He had under him various officers to carry out an elaborate system of checks and counter-checks on the goods leaving and arriving at the port by sea. There was the tide-waiter who was put on board a ship at the earliest opportunity to ensure that, as it made its way to a wharf, nothing was taken off before duty had been paid by the importer. Another officer was the landing-waiter who had to be constantly in attendance when a ship from foreign parts was being unloaded. He was accompanied by a landing-surveyor who supervised him.

Coal was the only article of importance on which duty had to be paid when it was moved coastwise. This duty was finally abolished in 1831 and up to that time a Customs official, called a coal meter, had the job of checking the weights of cargoes shipped in to ensure that the duty paid in advance by the importer was sufficient.

Strict regulations were enforced to make sure that duty had been paid on foreign goods imported and which were later shipped coastwise. Before this could take place the master had to apply for a permit, called a sufferance, specifying the contents of his cargo, and if it included foreign imports, a statement had to be made on oath that duty had been paid on them. On arrival at his destination the master handed over his sufferance to a Customs coast-waiter who checked it against the cargo and then entered the particulars of it, in great detail, in his sufferance books.

The officials at the appointed Customs Ports also had jurisdiction over smaller ports, classified as Creeks, which lay within the limits of a length of coastline allotted to them. In the eighteenth century St Ives was subservient to Penzance, but by 1762 it had been made a Customs Port in its own right with control over the coastline from the Brisons, off Cape Cornwall, to Chaple-an-Gather, Perranzabuloe. Hayle and Portreath were Creeks and the amount of Customs business that could be transacted at them was limited. Duties, for example, had to be paid at the head-port which was most inconvenient for the Hayle traders especially when ship movements in and out of the port increased. It was not until 1864 that Hayle was declared a Customs Port, a ranking which it lost in 1882.

With the extensive seaborne trade at Hayle, Customs officers were kept busy. As the coastwise shipment of coal was frequent a coal meter was stationed in the port to check on the cargoes. Among the witnesses who gave evidence in the St Aubyn/Sandys case over the East Quay rights in 1830 was one Silvanus Gibbs who said that he was employed, mainly at Hayle, as a tide-waiter and coal meter. Others so engaged at one time were Nathaniel Tom and James Wallis. Another Customs officer posted to Hayle as a landing-waiter in the 1770s was William Biggleston. In 1774 he married Anna Phillips at Phillack church. She was a descendant of the Rev Gregory Phillips, Rector of Phillack when Civil War broke out in 1642. Refusing to conform to the new religion of the Puritans he was ejected from his living, his possessions were confiscated and to escape further persecution he had to go into hiding. It was a rule, made for obvious reasons, that Customs appointments could not be made from local people and William Biggleston may have come from Devon. His descendants continued to live in Hayle and will have been known by many residents.

In 1839 George O'Neil was the tide-waiter at Hayle and in the 1850s William Henry Holmes was the officer-in-charge. By 1873, by which time Hayle was a Customs Port, James R. Pascoe was the Collector with Thomas Harris and James Henry Redfern. They were ranked as Examining Officers – classed before 1861 as landing-waiters – and examined imported goods for duty. As the years passed Customs officials of various ranks were stationed at Hayle and among them was Ernest Tyndale Pascoe a well-known figure around the port when he was the officer-in-charge in the 1920s and 1930s.

Among the witnesses in the St Aubyn/Sandys case referred to above was one, Richard Tredinnick who admitted when cross-examined on his evidence, that he was a smuggler and went out into St Ives Bay from time to time at night. He said he found his way back in the darkness by making for a light in one of the rooms of the Steampacket Inn, no doubt placed there for the purpose. Responsibility for putting a stop to Tredinnick's activities and many others with similar intent was the task – not always successfully accomplished – of the Customs Waterguard Service members of which liaised in their operations with their land-based colleagues.

The inconvenience of having the principal Customs officers resident at St Ives and for whose services a payment had to be made when they attended the discharge of timber ships at Hayle – 7/6 a day for the landing-waiter and 10/6 for the landing-surveyor – prompted Henry Harvey to apply to the Commissioners

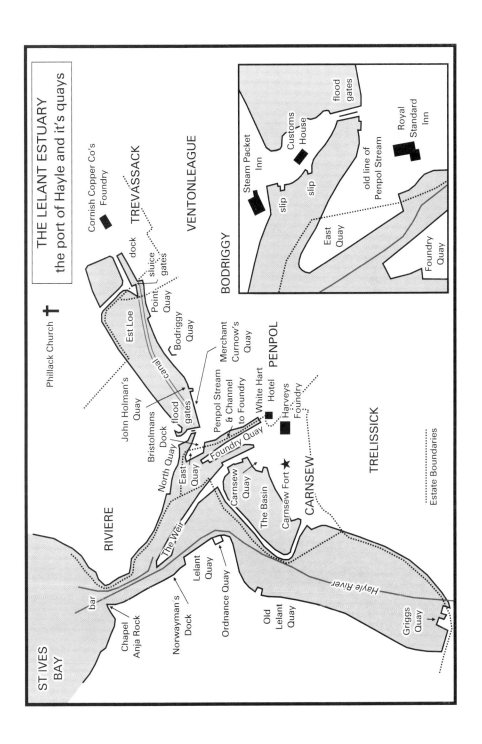

THE LELANT ESTUARY
the port of Hayle and it's quays

Cornish Copper Co's Foundry

TREVASSACK

VENTONLEAGUE

BODRIGGY

Steam Packet Inn

Customs House

flood gates

Royal Standard Inn

slip

slip

old line of Penpol Stream

East Quay

Foundry Quay

Phillack Church

dock

sluice gates

Point Quay

Bodriggy Quay

Est Loe

canal

John Holman's Quay

Merchant Curnow's Quay

Penpol Stream & Channel to Foundry

White Hart Hotel

PENPOL

Harveys Foundry

Bristolmans Dock

flood gates

North Quay

East Quay

Foundry Quay

TRELISSICK

RIVIERE

The Weir

Lelant Quay

Carnsew Quay

The Basin

Carnsew Fort

CARNSEW

Estate Boundaries

bar

Chapel Anja Rock

Norwayman's Dock

Ordnance Quay

Old Lelant Quay

Hayle River

Griggs Quay

ST IVES BAY

49

The weir at the entrance to Hayle Harbour.

Tree trunks marking the western side of the channel across Hayle Bar –
the approach to the port of Hayle.

For centuries a ferry service ran between Lelant and Hayle. The ferryman's house also provided a fine subject for numerous photographs and postcards over the years. Here Lelant Quay, now known locally as Dynamite Quay, is visible in the background behind the ferryhouse.

Here an unusual photograph shows boat hulks in use as homes.

Showing how treacherous Hayle Bar can be, the steamer S.S. *Hayle*, built by Harvey's of Hayle, aground on the sand of Hayle Bar close to the Black Cliffs. The crew were saved by Hayle's lifeboat c.1900 and the *Hayle* itself was later refloated by the salvage steamer *Lady of the Isles*.

Hayle's last lifeboat the *Admiral Rodd*. The boat was stationed in Hayle from 1906 until the Hayle RNLI station's closure in 1920.

Penpol Terrace. Note the horse-drawn railway to the right used for transporting goods from the Foundry area of town to East Quay.

The celebrations to launch a new lifeboat pass the Harbourmaster's office.

Sailing vessels alongside Hayle's quays.

Fore Street, Copperhouse.

The Copperhouse area of Hayle showing the canal with its walls made of black scoria block.

Looking across to the back of Hayle from Bodriggy, towards Clifton Terrace.

Taylor's Tea Rooms on Hayle Towans.

The Hayle Lifeboat launches. Note the 'Steam Packet Hotel,' the building on the left of the photograph.

Looking across Hayle's Foundry area towards Lelant Church, Knill's Monument and St Ives. Line drawing by the author's daughter Meryl.

Looking towards the North Quay slipway and Clifton Terrace.

Hayle power station and the quays and wharves of the port of Hayle beyond.

Cannon on Black Cliffs, Hayle Towans.

Aground in the distance is the S.S. *Fleswick* which ran aground on January 28th 1902 while carrying coal from Neath. Hayle's lifeboat the *F.H. Harrison* rescued all seven crew members and the *Fleswick* was later refloated.

A warship is towed up the Hayle channel towards Hayle harbour for scrapping.

Unloading cargo in Hayle Harbour in the early 1900s.
Note the horse-drawn wagons for transporting the goods.

Unloading cargo in the 1950s with the use of a motorised forklift.

The head of the Copperhouse Pool – Undercliff, Phillack.

The Hayle Regatta, held annually on Copperhouse Pool.

Hayle canal at the western end of Copperhouse Pool.

Location for swinging ships to exit Copperhouse sluice gates, Phillack Church Hall is on the right of the picture.

Copperhouse Mill, known as 'Paddy's Mill'.

The Copperhouse Mill's waterwheel, mill race and sluice gate with Phillack Church just visible in the background.

Hayle's swing bridge and main sluice.

A modern drilling platform in the approaches to Hayle Harbour looking towards Lelant. Note the house known as 'The Ferryhouse' behind.

of Customs in 1830 to be relieved of these charges. In support of his application he stated that no charge was made for the services of the officers who had to travel from Penzance when timber cargoes were unloaded at Marazion and St Michael's Mount.(41)

The extent of the inconvenience of the Customs arrangements at Hayle at this time may be gauged by the fact that it was sufficient to bring together, in peace for once, the old rivals Harvey & Company and the Cornish Copper Company. In 1836 they combined to petition the Lords of the Treasury to remove the Custom House from St Ives to Hayle. The basis of their plea, duly supported with evidence, was that many more vessels entered Hayle than St Ives. The St Ives counter-petitioners claimed that more vessels were owned by them than the Hayle merchants which was no doubt true, but in the circumstances, would seem to have been irrelevant. Nevertheless, Their Lordships decided that the Custom House should remain at St Ives(42) and four years later they were just as disobliging when they rejected a petition to allow a Bonded Store at Hayle for timber, flour, tea, coffee and sugar, as well as other merchandise for ships' stores.

Matters were not improved when St Ives was abolished as a Customs Port in 1860 and the coastline it controlled was added to the Port of Penzance with the result that the traders at Hayle and Portreath with Customs business to transact had even further to travel. At last, in 1864, following strong protests from all the interested parties, Hayle was constituted an independent Customs Port from 1 October. But it only remained so for a relatively short time as, in 1882, it was once again classed as a Creek under Penzance. Of the four Customs officers on duty at Hayle three were posted away and one – J. H. Redfern, Examining Officer – remained.(43)

In 1905 Hayle came under the Port of Falmouth and in 1925, under Plymouth with a Preventative Officer in charge until 1964 when the Hayle Custom House was officially closed though it was used up to 10 February 1979 by Customs Officers from Penzance to deal with such Revenue work as arose during the final years of the port's decline.

When Hayle was declared a Customs Port in 1864 it also became a Port of Registry for shipping. The registration of ships, as required by the Ships Registry Act of 1855, was carried out by the Customs officers and when Hayle ceased to be a Customs Port in 1882 its years as a Port of Registry also ended. From the Ships Registers of the Port of Hayle, published by the National Maritime Museum in 1975, we learn that seventy-six ships were registered or re-registered at Hayle. Of these, twenty-nine were built there.

The building which became the Hayle Custom House was erected by the Cornish Copper Company on the embankment which it made to form Copperhouse Pool. The lintel over the entrance door bears the date 1862.

Harbourmasters

AS FAR AS the movement of shipping is concerned the most important official in a port is the harbourmaster. Up to 1868, when Harvey & Company secured complete control of the port of Hayle with its purchase of the interests of the Cornish Copper Company, the supervision of the berthing of vessels and their departure was shared by the two companies. Thereafter, Harvey & Company appointed its own harbourmaster, the first being William Roberts who also acted as quay foreman.

The job of the harbourmaster at Hayle was one involving long hours as he had to be on hand whatever the time of day or night that ships arrived and sailed. He also had to liaise with the Trinity House pilots whose job it was to guide them into and out of the harbour. Then there were the boatmen to keep an eye on. In the days of sail they helped to warp vessels in and out and when sail gave way to the steam and diesel engine, one or two of them were still needed to give a hand with the ropes and assist generally as the ships berthed or got under way. Another important duty of the harbourmaster was to examine the state of the berths and to survey the channel into the harbour and the bar at its entrance to ensure that they remained navigable. During a spell of northerly gales, when there was much movement of sand, conditions on the bar and in the waterways could alter in a matter of hours. In due course, the water sluiced from Copperhouse Pool and the Basin brought conditions back to normal, but until that happened the harbourmaster had a duty to warn all concerned of the hazards. Another of his responsibilities was to ensure that the lights marking the channel and points in the harbour were lit as required during the hours of darkness.

Under the Explosives Act of 1875, Harvey & Company issued by-laws in 1883 (updated in 1928) for the discharge and shipment of explosives. The regulations were stringent and it was the harbourmaster's duty to enforce them. All sensible precautions had to be taken. No smoking was allowed; no iron studded boots could be worn; no drunkenness was permitted. The harbourmaster had to be informed in advance of the nature and quantity of the explosives to be shipped or discharged, the time of the movements and the quay to be used.

Among the harbourmasters at Hayle were:–
Richard Thomas in 1839 – Harvey & Company.
William Gilbert in 1861 – Cornish Copper Company.
Philip Biggleston Spray by 1872. He was a member of a well-known Hayle

family of seafarers and a master mariner like many of his relatives.

John Simons by 1880.

John Hampton by 1910.

George Boulden in the 1920s and early 1930s.

Capt. W. Q. Martin of Portreath and a former master of Harvey & Company's SS *Pulteney*, to 1943.

Capt. F. J. Webb, a native of Hayle and a master mariner with long service in foreign-going ships which was ended by enemy action in World War II, to 1955.

Capt. F. Lott, the master of a coaster and who knew Hayle harbour well followed Capt. Webb and continued into the 1960s.

Capt. F. Stamps succeeded Capt. Lott and during his service the shipping traffic in the port declined rapidly and he was the last full-time harbourmaster.

Working closely with the harbourmasters were the pilots and boatmen, many of whose families were long connected with the activities of the port. One such was the Love family, a member of which, Thomas, was a pilot in 1860 and another Hughie, a boatman and well-known local character, nearly a hundred years later.

Ship Agents, Lloyd's Agents and Vice-consuls

ON THEIR ARRIVAL in port ship-masters have many matters to attend to such as provisioning, pilotage, bunkering, repairs, the collection of cash and mail and sailing orders. To assist them with their requirements persons set up as ship agents in the various ports.

Up to the time when Harvey & Company became the sole operators of the port of Hayle it, and the Cornish Copper Company, acted as agents for their own ships and others carrying their imports and exports. After 1868 Harvey & Company had the monopoly of the ship agency business in the port apart from a short period in the late 1940s when a Penryn agent opened a branch office in Hayle.

Then there is the Lloyd's Agency. In 1811 the Committee of Lloyd's of London, the world famous marine insurers, decided to establish the Lloyd's Agency organisation in various ports with the prime duty of reporting to Lloyd's on shipping and other matters of interest to the Lloyd's insurance market. Among the most important of these are the daily movements of shipping and marine disasters when the agents became responsible for arranging surveys of the ship's hull and cargo when there was not a total loss.

Lloyd's Agents are allotted areas of responsibility and up to 1879 the port of Hayle was within the district of the St Ives Agent. In that year the Hayle Agency was established with coverage from the west of Hayle bar to St Agnes Head. This was extended to Gurnards Head when the St Ives Agency was disestablished in 1954.

The first Lloyd's Agent for Hayle was John Vivian, a director of Harvey & Company which held the Agency until December 1973 when, in a rationalisation of the United Kingdom Agencies, Hayle was disestablished and added to the district of the Plymouth Agency.

Vice-Consuls are appointed by foreign governments at ports regularly visited by ships of their nationals to give assistance to crew members in cases of emergency. A succession of members of the board of directors of Harvey & Company were Vice-Consuls for Norway and Sweden for many years.

Penzance (Hayle Division) Port Sanitary Authority

IN 1896, FOLLOWING legislation, the Hayle Division of the Penzance Port Sanitary Authority was set up.(44) The first members of the Board were F. Harvey, H. H. Trevithick, H. J. Warren, H. T. Broad, W. M. D. La Touche and F. Gilbert. The Clerk was Edward Boase and the Treasurer, R. F. Bolitho. The Medical Officer was Dr T. Mudge and the Inspector of Nuisances, G. H. Eustice.

The duty of the Medical Officer was to inspect the living accommodation on board vessels when there was evidence of a health hazard. He also had to deal with cases of infectious diseases on board vessels entering the port. If there happened to be any sickness among the crew and passengers of which the Pilots became aware when bringing a vessel into port they had to notify the Medical Officer immediately the ship berthed. When this became necessary with a night arrival, the Pilots received a special payment – in 1900 this was 2/6!

The Inspector of Nuisances was concerned with sanitary matters in the port such as the dumping of rubbish in the harbour. Another of his jobs was to dispose of stranded whales and seals in the harbour or on Hayle beach. For his salary of £5 per annum he was kept busy; for example, in the quarter to 29 September 1896 there were seventeen incidents which required his attention.

The sea, from time to time, claimed its victims in and near the port and for their temporary accommodation the Board had a mortuary built in the yard near the Royal Standard Inn.

The Trade Through the Port

ADEQUATE RECORDS ARE available from which the history of the material structure – the quays and so on – of the port of Hayle can be traced. On the other hand, the sources of information relating to the numbers of vessels using the port and the tonnages and descriptions of the commodities shipped in and out are sparse to start with, but become more numerous later on.

To get some idea of the type and volume of trade through the port in the late seventeenth century and in the eighteenth when it developed and expanded it is necessary to blend a knowledge of contemporary events with the fragments of information available.

In the Public Records Office there is a series of Port Books in which are recorded details of coastal and overseas trade. The contents of the books for Cornwall between 1600 and 1700, which have survived, have been analysed in great detail.(45) The books were kept to ensure that , as far as possible, the Crown received its full revenue from the Customs dues. At this time Hayle came within the Customs Port of St Ives and separate returns of its trade were not made. Shipped into St Ives were such basic materials as iron, agricultural implements and domestic ware, timber for building and other purposes, coal and a variety of manufactured goods such as grates, kettles, chimney backs and anvils. Although returned under St Ives in the Port Books a proportion of these goods would have been landed in the Hayle estuary in the seventeenth century towards the end of which Bodriggy Quay was built.

Among the merchants at St Ives named in the Port Books was a John Stephens and it was this man or his son who, in 1713, as already related, took a lease of two acres of land in Penpol and built a quay and stores there. He had probably been running his ships into Hayle for some years and had built up a good business which warranted its own premises. Among his customers could have been the proprietors of the Angarrack Tin Smelting House, established in 1704, which used large quantities of coal for its furnaces as did that of the older Treloweth Smelting House hardby the Lamb and Flag Inn at Canonstown. Another large consumer of coal near John Stephens' quay and stores at Penpol was a copper smelting works set up in 1710.

Up to the end of the seventeenth century the output of the copper mines in Cornwall was small, but in the early years of the next, their expansion began in earnest thanks to the introduction of the steam engine to pump water from them as the search for the ore went deeper. Surrounded by these mines on its landward side Hayle was well placed to provide a way in for the coal for their pumping engines and building materials such as timber, bricks, lime and iron. It was also a convenient place from which to ship to South Wales for smelting the copper ore not processed by the local smelters.

It is against this background provided by the mining industry that the trade of the port of Hayle developed during the eighteenth century. Hard facts and figures by which its growth can be measured are, as already explained, few for this period but it is possible to chronicle some significant events which must have stimulated trade from time to time.

1710   In this year a duty on coal carried coastwise and used for smelting was abolished. In the same year a copper smelting works was set up at Penpol which continued until 1735.

1716   About this time the first Newcomen steam engine was set up in Cornwall to pump water from a mine in Breage parish not far from Hayle. The Newcomen engine needed enormous quantities of fuel – up to five tons a day. The cost of this coal together with the import duty levied on it deterred mine adventurers from installing many more of them.(46)

1720   By now upwards of 6,000 tons of copper ore were being produced annually by the Cornish mines. Much of the ore came from those near Hayle, in particular Herland and Relistian in Gwinear and Binner Downs in Crowan. Some forty vessels were employed in carrying this ore to South Wales and bringing back coal, much of it through Hayle.

1739   The duty on coal imported into Cornwall from Wales for use in mine steam engines was abolished and this gave a boost to the installation of more Newcomen engines, some of which were erected at mines in the Hayle area. The abolition of the duty at this point was timely as the demand for Cornish copper was growing rapidly.

1746   John Holman built a quay at Penpol next to that of John Stephens and commenced to trade.

1750   The Lelant Brewery was established in the village and the old quay nearby was brought into use to receive cargoes of coal and barley.

1752   Steatite or soapstone, an important constituent in the manufacture of porcelain, was found in the Mullion area and shipped from Hayle to Liverpool.

1754   In this year the partners of the Cornish Copper Company, as it was later called, transferred their copper smelting operations from Camborne to Ventonleague and began to import all their coal requirements into Hayle.

1758   'Hayle is a place of considerable trade for iron, Bristol wares, but more especially Welch coal, for which at present there is such a demand for fire engines (pumping engines), smelting houses and the home consumption of the populous neighbourhood that usually there are about 500 and oftentimes 1,000 horses which come to carry off coals for some purpose or another, six days in the week. The fire engines which take off the greatest quantity of coal from this harbour are still increasing in number and trade here must reasonably advance.' (46)

It was reckoned that a mule or pack horse could carry about three hundredweights of coal or copper ore. Taking a figure of 750 animals on the move each day for six days indicates that some 1,350 tons of coal and copper ore passed through the port of Hayle in the course of a week though this volume would not have been sustained in the winter months when shipping delays were often lengthy because of bad weather and contrary winds.

1760   John Stephens, the pioneer merchant at Hayle in 1713, prospered in his undertaking and in the course of time took partners, among them William Lemon who made a fortune from mining and used his wealth to buy a stake in many a promising local surprise. He died in 1760 and an inventory of his assets was prepared and this shows what stock the partnership – then known as the Hayle Company – had at the time.(47)

The stock included:–   Coal, iron, lead, steel
Timber, bricks, lime, glass, nails
Colours (paints), pitch
Soap, salt
Shovels, grinding stones, scythes
Kettles and baking irons

Recognisable here are basic industrial materials and domestic ware which were sold to the company's customers of which there were 198 on its books at 31 March 1760. Of these, 27 accounts were with local mines. The company also owned a sloop, the *Prince George*, which would have spent much of its time between Hayle, South Wales and Bristol. Listed among the assets were tow lighters for use when the *Prince George* and any other vessel could not get alongside the company's quay for lack of water and had to be unloaded in the harbour.

The record of the prices at which stocks of the Hayle Company were valued in 1760 makes interesting reading. Coal, for example, was costed at 15/- per ton, equivalent to 9d per cwt. The debts owed to the company amounted to £4,236, nearly a half of it by mine adventurers who were notoriously slow to pay their bills. On the basis of three months credit and the cost of coal at 75p per ton in 1760, compared with what it is now, the company's annual sales must have approached a million pounds in present day values. The partners did well out of the business and one of them, John Curnow, who at first had the smallest share in it, was able, in 1770, to buy the freehold of the whole of the Bodriggy estate and part of Penpol for £3,000. He also bought out the interests of his co-partners in the Hayle Company which he sold to the Cornish Copper Company in 1778.

By 1793 there was a regular shipping service between Hayle and Bristol, the *John and Betsey*, the *Hayle Trader* and the *Bristol Trader* each visited the port once a month.(48) But as they had in the past, and would continue to do for many years to come, the imports of coal for the local mines and the shipment of their copper ore to South Wales for smelting, provided the base for the port's steady growth in terms of trade.

Busy Times

Some idea of the variety of goods entering Hayle and leaving it in the early years of the nineteenth century can be gathered from a summarised record, details of which appear in the Appendix. The information extracted from a Customs Sufferance Book relates to the year 1815 and excludes coal. In September 1817 as many as thirty-one ships arrived at Hayle during one week.

In 1829 there was a minor set-back. It has already been recounted how the Cornish Copper Company, in a fit of pique over the threatened loss of its East Quay, ceased to operate the sluice gates regularly for some time and in consequence the harbour silted up. When sluicing was resumed it was a year or two before all the accumulated sand was cleared and some time before larger vessels could use the port again. The result of this was that most of the timber trade was temporarily lost to other ports.(49)

The packet service between Hayle and Bristol continued as regularly as weather conditions permitted, but the year 1831 was notable for the introduction to the service of a steam vessel to replace the sailing ship *Albion*. The new packet was the wooden paddle steamer *Herald* which plied between the two ports carrying passengers and freight. The freight was mainly inwards at first and of a miscellaneous kind consisting of a range of foodstuffs for the local traders – butter, coffee, mustard, vinegar, pimento, flour, molasses and fruit. Building materials such as paint, putty, turpentine and nails were brought down from Bristol as well as tobacco, snuff, soap, serge and glue.(50)

The *Herald* was owned by the Hayle Steamship Company in which the Harvey family held shares. The company bought another steampacket, the *Cornwall*, which went into service on the Hayle/Bristol run in 1842. In May 1847 this vessel transported some 20,000 head of broccoli to Bristol. This trade was started in 1837 when a series of spring frosts destroyed the usual vegetable supplies available in Bristol, and Sharrock Dupen, the steward on the *Herald* took to the city a small quantity of broccoli which he quickly sold.(51) To Dupen, therefore, must go the credit for establishing a trade which, in the years ahead, became the mainstay of the Cornish farming industry.

In 1842 another packet steamer made its appearance on the Hayle/Bristol circuit. This was the *Brilliant* owned by Vivian Stevens of St Ives and which he transferred not long afterwards to a new company named the Brilliant Steampacket Company. Not to be outdone by their old rivals the Harveys, the partners in the Cornish Copper Company took shares in the new company. Competition between the packets became intense and gave a boost to the rivalry between the parties. Fares and freight charges were cut; the masters raced each other between the ports of Hayle and Bristol and bets were placed on them.(52) On one occasion, someone, in order to delay the *Brilliant*, cut off the labels on its packages which were then sent to the other packets! That was serious and a reward of £20 was offered for information leading to the detection and conviction of the culprit.(53) He does not appear to have been caught.

The convenience of travel to and from West Cornwall by the steampackets *Herald* and *Cornwall* attracted more than 7,500 passengers in 1845(54) and large numbers were also carried by the *Brilliant*. All these travellers going abroad or landing and making their way to continue their journeys by train or coach – maybe after taking refreshment at the Steampacket, Royal Standard or White Hart – presented a busy scene at Hayle in the middle of the last century. Many of those leaving the port were emigrants outward bound on ships sailing direct to their new country, or on their way to join ships at other ports of embarkation. Very few of those who bid them farewell on the quayside ever saw them again. To add to all this activity were the arrivals and departures of vessels laden with cargoes or in ballast. In 1845 there were no less than 734 of these carrying some 135,000 tons of goods of one kind and another but mainly coal and 28,000 tons of copper ore shipped to the smelters in South Wales.(55)

Unique exports from Hayle, from time to time, were the celebrated products of the engineering works of Harvey & Company and the Cornish Copper Company, mainly large pumping engines and all kinds of mining machinery shipped worldwide. As many of the parts were massive and very heavy, particularly the cylinders and beams of the engines, getting them aboard and stowing them safely for a long voyage was a delicate operation.

Now and again an unusual cargo would come into Hayle. In 1846 the local potato crop failed as a result of a disease, and to alleviate the shortage large quantities were shipped in from Rouen during the following year. The vessels usually berthed at the Bristolman's Dock, and the potatoes were quickly sold at the quayside.(56)

As time passed the steampackets *Herald*, *Cornwall* and *Brilliant* were replaced in succession by others – the *Express*, the *Cornubia* (built by Harveys and later to become a successful blockade runner during the American Civil War), *Queen*, *Albion*, *Bride* and *Bessie*. When Brunel's railway bridge over the Tamar was completed in 1859 and Cornwall was linked by rail to other parts of the country the days of the Hayle/Bristol packets were numbered and the last of them, the Bride was withdrawn in 1874.

One of the early Harvey sidelines was flour milling. The mill, of which little now remains, was at the foot of Foundry Hill. In 1852 the business was taken over by John Harvey Trevithick, a nephew of Henry Harvey and run as J. H. Trevithick & Sons. The firm imported into Hayle large quantities of grain from the Baltic and America and fruit from the Mediterranean countries which it shipped in its own vessels, the schooners *Jane Banfield* and *Kate* and the steamer *Richard Trevithick*.

In 1890 the Trevithicks joined forces with William Hosken, who milled at Loggans, and S. J. Polkinhorn of Truro, to form Hosken, Trevithick, Polkinhorn & Company Ltd (HTP). The Trevithicks had built up a large wholesale grocery business which was absorbed by the new company. It was the practice to bring the groceries down to Hayle by rail, but in 1893, dissatisfied with the high railway freight charges it had to pay, the company decided to have its own ship and bring its requirements from Bristol, Liverpool and elsewhere by sea. A storage shed was built on East Quay and a small steamer was bought and named *Snowflake* (after the company's own brand of self-raising flour). Not long after, this vessel was replaced by the larger *M.J.Hedley* which plied between Hayle, Bristol and Liverpool with general cargoes in addition to supplies for HTP. She had limited accommodation for passengers, and in a small way revived the old packet service. The *M.J.Hedley* was sold in 1917 and the general cargo service which she provided was suspended until after the war when it was restarted by Gilchrist & Company of Liverpool operating from East Quay. Gilchrist continued until 1935 and gave up then because of business losses. In the following year Coast Lines Ltd took over and its general cargo coasters were regularly routed to Hayle. Next on the scene came J. Bibby & Sons Ltd in 1952 for a few years and with the departure of that company Hayle's general cargo service came to an end.

Hayle Ahead

Going back a hundred years to resume our place in time we can get a glimpse, from the report of the Trinity House Pilots on their work in 1871,(57) as to how the shipping traffic into Hayle compared with that of other Cornish ports. The pilots took 543 vessels into Hayle and into Fowey, Mevagissey, Par and Looe 335, Padstow 338, Penzance 167, St Ives 107 and Portreath 91. Of the total, no less than 461 were steamers and nearly all of them came into Hayle. These figures show the pre-eminence of Hayle among the Cornish ports at this time.

Between 1878 and 1887 imports into Hayle averaged 112,911 tons annually and ranged in total from 93,822 tons in 1878 to 139,968 tons in 1887. The bulk of this tonnage was coal – 78,856 tons of it in 1878 rising to 111,356 tons in 1887. Other imports in this year were grain 18,419 tons, iron, dynamite, timber, slates, bricks, coke and manure.(58) In one week alone in November 1887 as many as twenty-six vessels came in. Coal was carried by twelve of them and grain by ten including four from Germany. Of the remaining four, two brought slates from Padstow, one dynamite from Briton Ferry and one a general cargo from Liverpool.(59)

From 1878 to 1887 exports from Hayle ranged annually from 13,976 tons to 11,938 tons and consisted mainly of copper ore, wolfram, tin, machinery, arsenic, china clay and flour. During the years between 1878 and 1887 the exports of copper ore fell (from 9,119 tons in 1878 to 6,004 tons in 1887) as did those of tin and arsenic which reflected the decline of the mining industry. On the other hand, the export of flour had been started by the millers, W. Hosken & Son, of Loggans, and in 1887, 4,235 tons were shipped out. The import trade received a boost in that year as the substantial coal business of Messrs Williams was transferred from Portreath to Hayle. In January 1887 the firm brought in 3,000 tons of coal and in one week sent 2,200 tons to the mines which prompted the local newspaper to comment that 'it was one of the busiest remembered for coal.' Most of the coal shipped in by Messrs Williams was carried in their own vessels, the *Lynx*, *Salisbury* and *Ogmore* – all steamers.(60)

When Harvey & Company took over the waterside premises of the Cornish Copper Company the use of the quays at Copperhouse was continued. The first Harvey vessel to go there was the *Henry Harvey* which, in March 1868, sailed up the canal in triumphant style with flags flying, into the heartland of the old enemy. Remembering Henry Harvey's years of struggle which led to this moment what better ship to carry the colours than the one that bore his name.

The quays at Copperhouse were used for many years. Coal was shipped in by Harvey & Company to the Dock; the last vessel to bring a cargo was the *Hayle* early in the twentieth century.(61) W. Hosken & Son used Point Quay for their imports of wheat, maize, oats and linseed cake and the export of flour.(62)

The china clay included in the exports from Hayle in the 1870s and 1880s came from the Tregonning Hills, but the deposits were not of good quality, and a partnership which took over the rights to exploit them started a profitable sideline by making firebricks from the clay.(63) Many of these bricks, along with clay, were exported to New York particularly in the barque *Charlotte Young* which would return with grain for J. H. Trevithick & Sons.(64) This ship was a frequent visitor to Hayle and for a time had the distinction of being a 'teetotal vessel'. The crew, following the example of the master Captain Crooks, when signing on for a voyage in March 1883, became members of the Blue Ribbon Mission the optimistic object of which was to put an end to the taking of strong drink.(65) Captain Crooks left the *Charlotte Young* in June 1883 and it must be a matter for speculation how long his old crew resisted temptation.

Hopes were raised in 1883 that china clay from the St Austell district might be railed to Hayle and shipped out as back freight in vessels which had brought in coal. But this was not to be as the Great Western Railway was not in favour of the idea and scotched it by quoting prohibitive freight rates between St Austell and Hayle.(66)

Between 1891 and 1915 an average of 523 ships used the port of Hayle annually, but after 1916 the numbers were reduced drastically because the war at sea restricted shipping movements.(67) Records of shipping for the port from 1902 - 1916 show that the tonnages of coal and grain were still dominant. In addition to coal for domestic purposes it was brought in for the few mines still in operation – Dolcoath, Levant, Bassett, East Pool and South Crofty – the local gasworks at Hayle, St Ives, Helston, Camborne and Redruth as well as the new Electric Power Station at Hayle. Nitrate of soda was imported in large quantities for the National Explosives factory at Upton Towans.(68)

For some time after the 1914 - 1918 war national trade was depressed, and this was reflected in the number of ships entering Hayle compared with the pre-war years even after allowing for the fact that they were able to carry larger tonnages. In 1923 the number was 253, but there was an improvement in the following year with 298, which was sustained, but not sufficiently to prevent the disposal by Harvey & Company of the *Hayle*, which had been laid up since 1921, after giving sterling service for nearly forty years. The company's

Pulteney, bought in 1916, was kept in use, as was the *Mellenear* launched in 1921, but they were both unprofitable until an upturn in trade came in 1925. Three years later the *Mellenear* was wrecked off Land's End and the sale of the *Pulteney* in 1933 marked the end of shipowning by Harvey & Company.

During the inter-war years the closure of most of the tin mines in the district resulted in a reduction of the imports of coal for them, but the tonnages in time were more than replaced by the increasing demands of the Power Station which was enlarged at intervals. Imports of petroleum products by the Anglo-American Oil Company, later the Esso Petroleum Company, also increased as did shipments of cement. The import of grain by HTP ended in 1931 when the company ceased to mill at Loggans.

The Second World War put a stop to the upward trend in the volume of the port's traffic, but in the years immediately following the end of it in 1945 there was another surge forward. The coal requirements of the Power Station increased very substantially as the demand for electricity for industrial and domestic purposes rose. By the early 1950s the station was burning some 150,000 tons of coal a year and required a shuttle service of vessels to maintain supplies. Notable ships on the South Wales/Hayle run at this time were the steamers *Avanville* and *Stanville* to be followed later by the newer diesel-engined coasters, the *Gardience*, *Kindrence* and *Nascence* owned by the London & Rochester Shipping Company.

Large quantities of domestic and gas coal were also imported and cement was much in demand to meet the increasing needs of the local building industry. Cement imports reached a peak of 8,862 tons in 1955 – twenty years previously it had been much less than half that total. The post-war increase in the number of motor cars, lorries, farm tractors and central heating installations pushed up the imports of petrol, diesel and heating oils, into the Esso depot on North Quay, to some 25,000 tons annually. On a smaller scale were shipments inwards of timber, potatoes, fertilisers and sulphur, this last for Associated Octel, and outwards, scrap metal from Foundry Quay and fuses from the ICI factory at Tuckingmill which were shipped from Lelant.

By 1959 the annual tonnage of shipments into and out of the port of Hayle exceeded 200,000 tons carried in some 550 shiploads. This level of activity continued well into the 1960s then the decline set in.

Supporting Industries

ATTRACTED BY THE facilities available a number of industries were established around the perimeter of the port of Hayle. It was as well that they were as they gave a new lease of life to the port at a time when the mining industry, on which it had depended for so long, had contracted.

The Electric Power Station

In 1899 with commendable foresight, John Mead, one of the Harvey directors, submitted to his colleagues a scheme to generate electricity on a commercial scale by means of turbines driven by the power of the water released from the Copperhouse and Carnsew Pools. The scheme was accepted and immediately investigated with the help of consulting engineers, but it was not carried out. It seems likely that this was because a sufficient flow of water from the pools could not be sustained for long enough and the daily sluicing arrangements, which were of paramount importance, might have been put in jeopardy. Ten years later, Hayle was chosen for an Electric Power Station to be equipped with a coal-fired generating plant. A site on the eastern edge of the harbour was selected and in 1910 the station was completed. It was extended from time to time as the demand for electricity increased and with it the need for more and more coal which was shipped from South Wales and discharged at a section of North Quay set aside for the exclusive use of the Power Station.

A surplus generating capacity nationally, led the Central Electric Generating Board to close a number of its small stations which were costly to run. The Hayle station was among them and its end came in 1973. Along with its 240 feet high chimney, which was a landmark for miles around, the station was demolished in 1981.

Oil Storage and Distribution

The growth in the demand for fuel and heating oils and petrol after the 1914 - 1918 war brought the Anglo-American Oil Company – later Esso – to Hayle in 1923. A depot with storage tanks was built in a disused quarry on the edge of North Quay. Supplies were brought in by sea and pumped direct from the ships into the tanks. The depot closed in 1981.

Shipbreaking[69]

At the end of the 1914 - 1918 war many of the warships of the Royal Navy were no longer required and a number of them were obsolete and fit only for scrap. Among those taking part in the scrapping programme was Thos. W. Ward Ltd of Sheffield and to carry out its work the company bought Lelant Quay in 1920, and in the same year rented a large section of Foundry Quay from Harvey & Company.

The warships scrapped by Wards were mainly destroyers and the work went on for some years. When the supply of naval ships ran out old merchant vessels were brought in and demolished, the largest of these being the 6,039 ton liner *Meltonian* in 1933.

Coaxing some of the larger ships through the harbour channels was no easy task and not without incident. Among the first to be scrapped was the cruiser *Bristol* and in July 1921, as she was being towed in, she fouled the electricity cable astride the harbour, and West Cornwall had a forty-eight hour power cut as a result. In the same month a tug bringing in a large destroyer lost control of it and the vessel blocked the harbour channel for several days.

The last ship to be broken up by Wards was an old destroyer, the *Salmon*, in 1937, but this did not end the long association of Thos. W. Ward with the port of Hayle. In 1946 the company once again made use of Foundry Quay for shipbreaking and continued for a few years until the end of 1950. During this time two British and one German submarine were among the vessels which were scrapped.

A steady export of industrial and domestic scrap metal from Hayle occurred in the 1950s and 1960s by Meyer, Newman & Company and Thos. W. Ward reappeared on the scene. The former occupied the northern end of Foundry Quay and it was during its tenure that a part of the quay, where the old archway had been, collapsed in 1963.

In the 1970s for a time shipbreaking was resumed but not on a large scale. A submarine or two and a few ancient Fleetwood trawlers were broken up.

Shipbuilding

Both the Cornish Copper Company and Harvey & Company built ships during the nineteenth century, the last and largest of them all being the cargo steamer *Ramleh* built by Harveys in 1891.

In early 1918 the Admiralty expressed an interest in using the harbour and disused foundry buildings for shipbuilding and repairs but before anything happened the war came to an end and with it the Admiralty's intentions.

There was a revival of shipbuilding, but of a very different nature in 1943 when the premises on Foundry Quay previously used by Thos. W. Ward were taken over to build small naval vessels for the Admiralty. Landing craft for tanks and troops taking part in the Allied invasion of Europe in 1944 were built on the weir opposite Foundry Quay.

The Bromine Factory(70)

One of the essential components of high octane aviation spirit is ethylene dibromide which is manufactured from bromine. Before the last war the bromine requirements of this country were all imported, and a particularly important source was Germany. When war with that country appeared inevitable an alternative home-based source for a supply of bromine was sought with great urgency. It was found that only salt water could provide it in sufficient quantities and the warmer the water the better. Tests showed that the seawater around the Cornish coast was the warmest, and at Hayle a constant and very large supply could be obtained by taking the water after it had been used as a coolant by the Electric Power Station. In co-operation with ICI Ltd, which was entrusted with the construction of the factory, the supply of water, which hitherto had been drawn from the harbour, was obtained from Carnsew Pool through a tunnel driven under the bed of the harbour.

By the middle of 1940 the construction of the works had been completed on a site near the Power Station and ICI Ltd began to operate it in collaboration with the British Ethyl Corporation, later to become the Associated Ethyl Company Ltd. After the war the latter company – in due course to be named the Associated Octel Company Ltd – bought the factory from the Government.

In addition to its use to improve the octane level of commercial petrol to aviation standard by means of the ethyl dibromide manufactured from it, bromine is used in the chemical and pharmaceutical industries. The bromine was dispatched from Hayle, direct from the factory by rail, as was ethyl dibromide, some of which was exported to Australia, South Africa, India and Pakistan. By ship into Hayle came large quantities of sulphur needed in the manufacturing process.

The bromine factory continued in operation for some years after the war ended and it was closed down in 1973.

Glassworks

Although it had little effect on the economy of the port, as one of the industries in it at one time, the Glassworks deserves notice. It was built in 1917 on a site very near the Electric Power Station where it had access to the nearby sand necessary for the manufacturing process and which contained a high proportion of lime which made it suitable for glass making. Silica, the other essential ingredient was obtained from St Austell china clay waste. Both the sand and the silica had a high iron content so that the bottles manufactured were dark in colour.(71)

The owner of the glassworks was the Cornish Glass Company which went into liquidation in 1920 and the works were taken over by the Pentewan Glass Bottle Company. A new furnace was installed which was large enough to make ten tons of glass at a time. Operations continued for about five years until 1925. When the lease of the Steampacket Hotel expired in 1917 it was decided that the use of the property as a hotel should cease and it was let as offices for the Cornish Glass Company and later its successors until 1925.

Milling

There had been a number of small mills for grinding corn in Hayle and two of them, Loggans Mill owned by W. Hosken & Son and Foundry Mill by J. H. Trevithick & Sons, were enlarged and powered by steam in the 1880s. They were then able to produce and export flour on a large scale and in the years that followed thousands of tons of grain were imported into Hayle from other parts of England, the continent and America. This continued until Loggans Mill was closed in the 1930s, Trevithicks' Mill having ceased operations at the turn of the century.

Profit and Loss

THE PORT OF Hayle was developed so that full advantage could be taken of the commercial opportunities offered by the mining industry and the local community. As a result of the high cost of keeping the harbour navigable, the lack of statutory authority to levy harbour dues, and in the early days, the competition between the Harveys and the Cornish Copper Company, the profits made by the developers in operating the port were such that it was not a commercial success.

The capital cost of development was high. It is not known how much John Stephens laid out in 1713 to build his short length of quay or what the Cornish Copper Company spent on forming the Copperhouse Pool with its floodgates and embankment in the late 1780s. This scheme took three years to complete and must have been a costly undertaking even though the embankment was built of slag waste from the company's copper smelting works.

Foundry Quay was built in 1818 and cost the Harveys £9,000 with the aid of a loan from their bankers to whom interest had to be paid. East Quay constructed about the same time cost the Cornish Copper Company some £5,000. The expenditure on the Basin in 1833/4 was reckoned as £7,000 which Henry Harvey had to meet with another loan. Taking the average weekly wage in those days of about £1 and an increase of more than a hundredfold since then, it is apparent that in today's terms the amounts spent in the 1810s and 1830s by Henry Harvey and the Cornish Copper Company were enormous. Lelant Quay was built by the Trustees of the Tyringham estate in the 1870s for £16,000 and it was estimated that by 1883 Harvey & Company had laid out £100,000 on its quays, which included the amount paid for the former Cornish Copper Company property.(72)

The revenue of the port consisted of a charge to ships using it in the form of harbour dues and wharfage dues on goods stored on the quays before or after shipment.

Although the legal owner of the county's foreshores was the Duchy of Cornwall, the Praeds of Trevethoe in the eighteenth century, by virtue of their title to the lordship of the manor of Lelant and Trevethoe, claimed rights over all the harbour including the power to charge dues on vessels using it. By the end of the century the owners of the estates of Carnsew and Riviere, on which the harbour also abutted, asserted their assumed foreshore rights and the Praeds' share of the dues was reduced to three quarters of the total collected. The remaining one quarter was shared by the owners of Carnsew and Riviere. The dues were collected by the Cornish Copper Company and the Harveys and passed over to the landlords and all that the developers of the port received was a small commission. The total dues collected annually was trifling, never being more than about £50 as the charge right up to 1922 was only 1/6 per vessel regardless of size. The Trustees appointed under the St Ives Pier Act were more fortunate. In 1766 this Act was passed to permit the building of Smeaton's Pier in the harbour of St Ives for the better protection of vessels using the port and it authorised a charge to them of 1/4 per net registered ton to repay the cost of the construction of the pier and its maintenance. At this time the Port of St Ives officially included Hayle which was classed as a Creek and vessels entering also had to pay the 1/4 per ton dues. This inequitable charge, which brought in much more than the landlords' impost of 1/6 per vessel, continued until 1837 when the St Ives Pier Act was repealed following representations made by the Cornish Copper Company, Henry Harvey and others. From 1838 the Hayle dues became 2/6 per vessel at a wharf or 1/6 if at anchorage. This was a welcomed overall reduction which resulted in an increase in the number of ships using the port.

Without the power which a Hayle Harbour Act would have conferred the ability to make a charge for dues to help offset the cost of maintaining the harbour was questionable. Nevertheless, in 1871 by which time Harvey & Company had become the sole operators in the port, a buoyage charge was made of 3/- per vessel in addition to the harbour dues of 2/6. The new fee may have covered the cost of caring for the channel buoys, but not much else. These modest levies continued in force for many years and proposals were made in 1903 to replace them with one of 5d per net registered ton, but they were not adopted then and it was 1922 before they were. By this time the foreshore rights of the Duchy of Cornwall had been bought and were in possession of Harvey & Company as were the harbour due rights of the Trevethoe and Carnsew estates. In the years that followed the dues were gradually increased, but only with the consent of the Board of Trade. Although the increases were modest they invariably met with protests from shipowners. From time to time the floodgates had to be extensively repaired and on occasion replaced which meant an expenditure quite unrelated to current income.

If the net profits from the harbour operations were negligible or non-existent in the early years those resulting from the wharfages dues on goods stored on the quays were not much better. Before Henry Harvey built his Foundry Quay in 1818, the Cornish Copper Company, which up to that time had the monopoly of the available quay space in the port charged the smelters of South Wales 8d per ton for storing their ores before shipment and did very well out of it – about £1,000 a year it was reckoned.(73) To prevent Henry Harvey getting any business for his new quay the Cornish Copper Company suspended its wharfage charge for many years after 1818. Although it benefited the Welsh copper smelters this competition was disastrous for the antagonists at Hayle.

In reviewing the situation at length in about 1863, one of the Harvey partners showed how inadequate the revenue from their port operations had been during the previous forty-five years in relation to the expenses. He noted the effect of his company's 'liberal policy adopted by allowing local shopkeepers, traders, millers, grocers and tin smelters to import their requirements free of charge and how the great broccoli trade, now self-supporting, was fostered in this way.'(74) How the rival Cornish Copper Company fared in the same period of forty-five years is not known as its records have not survived, but the conclusion must be that its profits from that part of the port which it controlled were equally small. After 1868, when Harvey & Company became the sole operator in the port its profits from wharfing improved, but it is true to say that for most of its existence as a port its cost of development and keeping it open was subsidised by the engineering and trading activities of the Cornish Copper Company and Harvey & Company.

The Hayle Lifeboats

WITH GALE FORCE winds blowing from the north, St Ives Bay was no place to be, but many ships were caught there in such weather when waiting for the tide to rise enough for them to enter Hayle harbour. In these conditions they were sometimes driven ashore with dragging anchors to become wrecks with little chance of survival for those on board.

The nearest lifeboat was at St Ives, the little six-oared *Moses*, which was quite inadequate for crossing the Bay in a violent storm. As the number of vessels entering Hayle increased so did the casualties and, in 1866, the Royal National Lifeboat Institution stationed a lifeboat there.(75) This was bought with funds raised at Oxford University and named *Isis*, and before being brought to Hayle at the expense of the Great Western Railway Company, the boat had the distinction of being taken to Oxford and tried out by the 1866 University crew.

The *Isis* was in service until 1887 when it was replaced by the *New Oriental Bank* which was renamed the *E.F.Harrison* after one of the founders of the bank in whose memory it was given by the staff. This boat remained on station until 1906 when it was replaced by the third and last lifeboat at Hayle – the *Admiral Rodd*, the gift of Mrs W. M. Rodd of Tunbridge Wells.

The Hayle Lifeboat Station was closed in 1920 and from 1866 the three boats made forty service launches and during twenty-nine of these, saved ninety-five lives. The work of rescue by the Hayle lifeboat was confined to the waters of St Ives Bay with one notable exception. During a tempestuous night in January 1895, the steamer *Escurial*, bound for the Adriatic with a cargo of coal, battered and out of control, finally ran aground off Portreath. Calls went out for the assistance of the St Ives, Newquay and Hayle lifeboats but only the *E.F.Harrison* reached the scene after being hauled overland from Hayle. After great exertions the lifeboat was launched into the mountainous seas, but after rescuing one man, it was thrown back on to the beach and the rescue attempt had to be abandoned. From the crew of the *Escurial* there were seven survivors.(76)

The Hayle lifeboat was housed in a building erected in the old quarry where the Esso depot was later sited. It was launched from a slipway made near the Custom House.

Defence

HARBOURS ARE CONVENIENT places for enemy troops to land in times of war, particularly if they were unprotected, so when an invasion was threatened building up their defences becomes of paramount importance.

Mention has been made of the 'cliff castle' at Carnsew. This site has not been excavated so there is no archaeological evidence of its age but ancient it must be. Overlooking and dominating the Hayle estuary its position must have been a defensive one against raiders by sea many centuries ago.

According to tradition another fortress lies beneath the sands on the eastern side of the harbour entrance.(77) The occupant, Teudor, is thought to have opposed landings by the Irish missionaries in the fourth century.

During the Tudor period England was continually at odds with continental countries and during the early years of the reign of King Henry VIII the coast of Cornwall was practically defenceless against pirates and foreign ships of war. Not until the end of the reign was much done to protect it. There were already two blockhouses at St Ives and probably others on the north coast, but the main effort to fortify was made on the more vulnerable south coast where the Pendennis and St Mawes castles were built in the 1540s to protect Falmouth harbour.(78)

In the reign of Elizabeth I England and Spain were often in conflict and in 1567 there were fears that a strong Spanish army stationed in the Netherlands might be used to invade this country. Lists were made of all men in the county over 16, and of the weapons and armour they could provide if called upon to repel an enemy attack. Details of this muster have survived.(79) In the event no invasion took place and the men of Phillack, St Erth and Lelant, who would have had to defend Hayle harbour and its neighbourhood, were allowed to stand down.

Twenty years later there was another threat to the country when Philip of Spain dispatched his Armada in an attempt to invade in 1588. This time we were better prepared to resist the Spaniards as a plan of Devon and Cornwall, 'as they were to be fortified in 1588 against the Landing of an Enemy', shows lines of barricades surrounding the Hayle estuary and the coast of St Ives Bay and orders were issued as to who should man them.(80)

Although the defeat of the Armada put an end to a possible Spanish invasion on a large scale the chance that there might be minor landings remained. One such occurred in 1593 when a party of Spaniards raided Paul, Mousehole and Penzance, and against little resistance set fire to buildings and generally made a nuisance of themselves. Next day, they were driven off, but it transpired that their intention was to do more damage along the shores of Mount's Bay and also to make for St Ives and Padstow with similar intent.(81) Had the Spaniards succeeded in making their way into St Ives Bay a landing in the Hayle estuary would have been a distinct possibility. With little to ravage on the Phillack side where there were only a few scattered farmsteads and a cluster of houses around the church at that time, Lelant, which was more developed, could have been in trouble. It was as well that the poorly armed locals were not put to the test against the seasoned raiders from Spain.

Another nuisance, to shipping this time, was the number of French privateers which, in the mid-eighteenth century, were very active along the Cornish coast. The losses to the merchants of the various ports, including St Ives, were such that they petitioned the Admiralty to station a guard boat in Mount's Bay to convoy and protect shipping.(82) This protection would have been welcomed at Hayle where the coastwise trade was increasing substantially at this period.

In 1778 England was once again threatened with an enemy invasion when France and Spain joined forces with America against it. As before, there was much activity to defend the county and the Cornish Militia was embodied, and in the following year the Regiment of Volunteers was formed and John Knill raised a company at St Ives for the defence of the town and neighbourhood.(83) This latest threat like those before it came to nothing, but these were uneasy times and in 1782 a battery of cannon was mounted on the cliff at Portreath to ward off a possible landing by the French.(84) Similar armament, probably placed there at the same time, is shown in a photograph taken at the Black Cliff on Hayle Towans in 1902. During the 1914 - 1918 war a number of ships were torpedoed in the approaches to St Ives Bay by German U-boats which were known to sneak right into the Bay at times and to fire at any that came within range field guns were sited on the Black Cliff.

By 1797 Napoleon Bonaparte had conquered most of western Europe and soon after was poised for his invasion of England which once again looked to its defences. Hayle's contribution to local defence was a corps of two companies raised in 1798 and called the Copperhouse Infantry Volunteers officered by R. Edwards and R. O. Millett, captains; J. Tippett and T. Ellis, lieutenants and J. Ellis and H. Huthnance, ensigns.(85) Because their work was considered to be of such national importance tin miners were exempt from military service under the Stannary Laws unless summoned for the purpose by their Lord Warden. The situation was so serious in 1798 that his call went out to tin miners aged between fifteen and sixty 'to engage themselves to be armed, arrayed and trained for the Defence of the Realm'. From the maritime parishes of Phillack, Gwithian, St Erth, Lelant and St Ives, where landings by the enemy might have been attempted, there were 238 volunteers able to arm themselves with a variety of weapons.(86) Fortunately, there was no invasion, but following Napoleon's escape from Elba, and just before his final defeat at Waterloo in June 1815 the fear of it was revived. William Hosken, of Loggans Mill, as a boy and then living in Lelant, well remembered the consternation in the village and the visit of an Army recruiting party complete with fife and drum.(87)

At the end of 1859 Europe seemed to be moving yet again towards war and as a precaution Volunteer Artillery Batteries and Rifle Corps were raised to defend the country's ports if it became necessary. At Hayle the 8th Duke of Cornwall's Artillery Volunteers and the 15th Duke of Cornwall's Rifle Volunteers were formed in 1860.

During the war years between 1939 and 1945 the arrangements for the defence of the Hayle estuary were similar to those made in the days of Philip of Spain and Napoleon. The defenders then can be likened to the Home Guard of 1940 with its patrols and defence positions built at strategic points around the harbour. Of vital importance was the bromine factory on North Quay producing an essential ingredient of aviation spirit not obtainable elsewhere during wartime. This was a prime target for attack, both from the air and the sea, and to protect it North Quay was guarded by Army units; boom defences were erected at all the quays and anti-aircraft guns ringed the neighbourhood.

Of interest is a series of maps of the country (now held at the Westcountry Studies Library, Exeter with a copy of the Hayle area at the Cornish Studies Library, Redruth), prepared by the Germans and based on our Ordnance Survey Maps. On these, by means of symbols, no less than fifty-eight different types of civil and military installations were pinpointed as targets of importance.(88) At Hayle seven installations were noted but not the bromine factory which was built after the Germans gathered the information for their maps in the days before the war started. Because of its importance this was just as well as it must have saved the factory from being singled out as a target for a special and determined air attack which might have destroyed it.

Hayle Regatta

MOST SEAPORTS HELD an annual regatta and Hayle was no exception. The event was staged for over 150 years from 1837 but not continuously. In the early days the competition in the races was provided by the local seamen in their working craft and later, events for pleasure yachts were introduced as well as swimming matches. Regatta Day, with a band playing, a fair, market stalls and general jollifications, provided an annual holiday for the participants and spectators alike.

The *Penzance Gazette* of 20 September 1843 carried an advertisement for a regatta to be held on the following Monday. Races were arranged for sailing boats, two-oared boats, four and six-oared gigs and there was also to be a sculling match. A band was to be in attendance and the day was to end with a dinner for fifty of the prominent locals at the Commercial Inn.

The venue for the Hayle Regatta was the Copperhouse Pool which provided a good course for the competitors and an ideal setting for the spectators who could watch the races from its banks or get a grandstand view from Clifton Terrace and the sloping path leading to it.

Between 1853 and 1869 no regattas were held, probably through lack of support though the strained relations between the Cornish Copper Company and Harvey & Company may have had something to do with it. They would have had to co-operate for the event as the Cornish Copper Company at that time had control over the water in the Copperhouse Pool and the participants as employees of both companies would all have needed time off on the same day. It is significant that very soon after Harvey & Company acquired the Copperhouse Pool, and control in the port generally, Hayle Regatta was revived in September 1870 and sponsored by the company. Its principal partners were closely involved in the organisation and supervision of the events and the engineering works and other parts of the business were closed for the day. The regatta was reported upon at great length in the local newspaper,(89) and it seems that its revival was a great success, the races being watched by 'thousands of spectators', many on a visit for the day and the weather was 'all that could be desired'. The great day was enlivened throughout by the band of the Hayle Artillery Volunteers and rounded off, as darkness fell, with a firework display and then a supper for the officials and their guests at the White Hart.

Races were held for two-oared and four-oared boats, four-oared and six-oared gigs, ships' boats, skiffs, sailing boats and lifeboats. The race between the lifeboats was the great event of the day. Four boats took part, from Sennen,

Penzance, St Ives and Hayle. After a hard-fought race around a two mile course the winner was the Sennen boat which, with a final desperate spurt, just managed to beat the Penzance men by two feet. The Hayle boat, sad to relate, came in last. As she was described as being not as 'well manned' as the others this was not unexpected. The first prizes for the race winners ranged between £1.15s and 10/- except for the lifeboats, which was £8, to make it worthwhile bringing them from a distance.

The four-oared boat and the six-oared gig races produced some acrimony between their crews. In the first, there was an argument over the placings at the start and in the second, the runners-up, narrowly beaten by a foot, protested that the coxswain helped the oarsman at stroke. 'Amid the storm of words' the judges could reach no satisfactory conclusions and the results were allowed to stand. Such incidents as these were not unknown at regattas held at Hayle in much later years.

Races between gigs from various ports were popular events at regattas held in the county and the boats were taken long distances to compete. The gigs were used by pilots for rescue work and fishing, and even smuggling trips to France. One gig well known on the regatta circuit was the *Treffry* of Newquay, built in 1838. When she was raced at Hayle in 1893, her crew, after leaving work on a Friday afternoon, rowed the twenty-two miles to Hayle bar which they reached just as the harbour was being sluiced. As a result the hardest part of the row was from the bar to the Copperhouse Pool at which they arrived at 11pm and then had to search for lodgings for the night.(90)

The 1914 - 1918 war put an end to Hayle Regatta for a time, but it was revived afterwards. The programme of events at the one held on 25 August 1934 showed fewer kinds of boats competing; gone were the ships' boats and the gigs, and the sailing boats were pleasure craft. There were races for five-oared whalers which were somewhat similar to gigs and the coxswains were expressly allowed to assist the stroke oars. It would seem that the fuss raised on this point in 1870 was remembered! A motorboat race was a feature in 1934 and not long afterwards powerboats made their appearance. Very light craft with outboard motors, they added a touch of excitement as they dashed around the course set for them at great speed, overturned at times and contrasted oddly with the sedate sailing boats.

The 1939 - 1945 war brought the annual event to another halt, and although hampered by the reduced depth of water in the Copperhouse Pool brought about by silting, it has since then, been held from time to time, but not on the scale of previous years.

Decline

IN TERMS OF tonnages handled the peak years of activity in the port of Hayle were in the 1950s and early 1960s. During this time annual shipments in and out and carried by some 550 vessels regularly reached the 200,000 ton mark.

In 1955 the South Crofty tin mine replaced its steam pumping engines with electric pumps. The coal for these engines had long been imported through Hayle. The port's development was founded on the mining industry and, the loss of the South Crofty business, though not of great consequence in itself, may be seen in retrospect as marking the beginning of the port's decline.

Another import that ended not long afterwards was coal for the local gasworks when the production of gas was concentrated at the larger works in the county, and from which it was distributed by a grid system of pipelines. For decades cement had been shipped into Hayle from Kent in increasing quantities, but when a cement works was built at Plymstock in 1967 it was brought down by road and rail and the seaborne traffic to Hayle came to an end.

With the construction of new coal and oil fired and nuclear power stations in the late 1950s and in the 1960s demands on the elderly Hayle Electric Power Station, where generating costs were higher, declined and reached a point where it was only required to generate at its former high level in times of exceptional national demand. This decline in the output of electricity at Hayle was matched by a gradual reduction in the consumption of coal which, in some previous years, had amounted to as many as 150,000 tons annually and accounted for a very large proportion of the port's total shipments.

In the early 1970s the Harvey domestic coal business was sold to J. H. Bennetts Ltd of Penzance. Although the tonnages brought in had been declining for some years in the face of competition from other forms of heating, they were still substantial, and shipments into Hayle continued.

In 1973 the Associated Octel bromine factory ceased operations and so ended the import of sulphur. By this time the shipment of cargoes of scrap metal outwards and timber and potatoes inwards had begun to fade away. In 1972 the number of ship arrivals at the port had declined to 164.

Coinciding with the port's shipping decline came difficulty in keeping the waterways and bar clear of sand by the time-honoured method of sluicing. Opinions differed both as to the reasons for this and the best way to deal with it. As to the reasons, it was known from long experience that in the course of a tide backed by a high north-west wind the amount of sand deposited on the bar and in the harbour channel could be enormous. In the past such deposits had eventually been flushed away by sluicing. The Carnsew and Copperhouse Pools had silted up over the years and as a result of this the sluicing power of the impounded water when released had become much less effective. Add to this the prolonged spells of north-west winds which occurred and brought in large quantities of sand, day after day, and perhaps we have the answer to the silting problem.

In an attempt to restore navigability which sluicing had failed to do, a method of scraping thousands of tons of sand from the channel was tried. This was effective for a time, but before long new deposits appeared and the sand was scraped out again – in all five efforts were made with giant earthmoving equipment which cleared some 12,000 tons on each occasion. An effort was also made to remove the unwanted deposits by pumping them ashore but again, any success was temporary. Clearly, the sea was winning the battle. Dredging the bar and channel was also tried, with limited success and it was accompanied by a change in the configuration of the entrance to the harbour and severe erosion of the sandbanks on either side of it. Some thought that this was the direct result of the dredging operations and others that the change was caused by the natural action of the sea.

When the silting problem became acute there was hope that, if oil was discovered off the Cornish coast, some use might be made of the port to service the drilling rigs. In the event, this expectation faded and with it the extra incentive to keep the port open. But coal for the Power Station and J. H. Bennetts Ltd and oil for the Esso depot were still required.

In spite of the efforts to keep the bar and the channel navigable for coasters a stage was reached where shipowners became reluctant to put their vessels at risk by using the port and this heralded its closure. The Power Station was declared redundant and closed down in 1976; J. H. Bennetts Ltd made more use of the port of Penzance and road transport and Esso disposed of its small tankers, which were costly to run, and supplied its depot by rail until its closure in 1981.

With the mining industry which gave rise to its development no longer using it; without those industries that came later to keep it in business and with no immediate possibility of their replacement, the port of Hayle was finally closed to coastal shipping in 1977. Now, the quays remain as a crumbling monument to the men who planned and built them. With the floodgates unused, the sea, unopposed is free to reduce the harbour to its near useless condition of centuries ago.

When the closure of the port came in sight in 1977 much belated local interest was aroused. Members of the Penwith District Council, the Hayle Parish

Council and the Hayle Chamber of Commerce had their say. The Hayle Harbour Users Association was formed for the purpose of reinforcing the attempts to keep the port open.

The UBM Group of Bristol, which in 1969 acquired Harvey & Company, the longtime owners of the port of Hayle, having decided to sell the property, placed it on the market in 1981. It was eventually bought in 1983 by Tekoa Hayle Limited which soon announced plans to reopen the harbour for commercial and leisure use and to build a small marina. Other proposals were made which would have the effect of revitalising the town. Apart from some dredging of the harbour channel little was done by Tekoa and a position of stalemate was reached in respect of the company's 'master plan' for the harbour area, and its implementation.

A New Deal for Hayle

DESPITE THE CLOSURE of the port of Hayle to coastal vessels in 1977, the number of fishing vessels using it steadily increased, though the level of navigational safety continued to decline. It was this deterioration which was blamed for the loss of three lives in February 1988 when the crabber *Gillian Clare* capsized on the bar in heavy seas when attempting to re-enter the harbour.

Public concern about this tragedy and the inaction of Tekoa, the harbour owners, prompted the Hayle Parish Council to approach Mr Peter de Savary, a noted entrepreneur, who had bought and transformed neglected Land's End and the moribund ship-repair yard at Falmouth, and ask him if he would consider purchasing Tekoa's property and develop it. Mr de Savary's reaction to this invitation was prompt and positive as he proceeded to buy it and later, Riviere Farm, the site of the old electricity works and the White Hart Hotel.

An office for the newly formed Hayle Harbour Company Limited was set up in the Old Custom House under the management of Mr Richard Roberts and immediate steps were taken to improve the navigability of the harbour by installing navigation lights and buoys. Then followed the unveiling of plans for the development of the property for commercial and residential purposes, leisure facilities, and above all, further improvements for the safety and convenience of the fishing fleet. These were to be effected by dredging the harbour channel and sluicing it regularly from water to be impounded in an area of the harbour between the end of North Quay and the weir by means of a barrage fitted with lock gates to enable vessels to pass to and from the quays, and new sluice gates on the seaward side of the Carnsew Pool.

Mr de Savary's plans for Hayle were so extensive that it decided that an Act of Parliament was essential in order to carry them out. In November 1988, an application was therefore made to introduce a Bill to establish the Hayle Harbour Company Limited as a harbour authority and to confer certain powers to enable it to operate Hayle harbour as a public harbour undertaking, to construct works in the harbour and for other purposes.

The Bill was unopposed by the House of Lords in May 1989, but met opposition in the House of Commons, mainly over conservation issues raised by the Royal Society for the Protection of Birds and the Nature Conservancy Council. These matters having been satisfactorily resolved, it was expected that the Bill would pass through the House of Commons without further delay, but during its second reading there were two last-minute objections, one by Mr Robin Corbett MP for Erdington because of his dislike for the Hayle proposals, and the other, by Mr Andrew Bennett MP for Denton and Reddish as a protest against the Private Bill procedure. When convinced of the need for a safer harbour at Hayle, and to restore the prosperity of the town, Mr Bennett withdrew his objection to the Bill as did Mr Corbett on condition that a ballot of Hayle residents was held to enable them to express their views on the proposed developments. The Bill then became the Hayle Harbour Act on the 27 July 1989, some 188 years after the first unsuccessful attempt was made by the Cornish Copper Company to establish Hayle as a statutory port.

The next move was to obtain planning permission to carry out the proposed development of the harbour area, and this was given by the Hayle Parish Council and the Penwith District Council. On the other hand, the Cornwall County Council stubbornly refused to accept the plans on the grounds that 316 of the houses that it was proposed to build would exceed the number permitted under the County Structure Plan. The need to build these houses was essential to provide funds towards the cost of the development of the harbour and without them the whole scheme was in jeopardy. Fortunately, the County Council's objection was over-ruled by the Secretary of State for the Environment in November 1990, without a Public Enquiry.

During the eighteen months it took to obtain the necessary planning approvals for the referendum on the proposals for Hayle, as demanded by Mr Corbett for withdrawing his objection to the Hayle Harbour Bill, a ballot was held and it resulted in an overwhelming vote of approval. The way was then clear for Mr de Savary to proceed to implement his plans through his company Aldersgate Developments.

Reading about the numerous obstacles faced by Mr de Savary in his attempts to restore the fortunes of Hayle and revitalise it as a fishing port, as featured from time to time in the *Cornishman*, (the reports in which, I acknowledge in describing this latest phase in the history of Hayle), one is reminded of the town's earlier entrepreneurs, the partners of the Cornish Copper Company and John Harvey and his son Henry, and their efforts to develop the port of Hayle. Though they did not have to contend with planning authorities and the need to satisfy the demands of the conservationists, environmentalists and other interested bodies, through their implacable rivalry they created formidable difficulties for themselves in their attempts to thwart each others plans.

History shows that it has rarely been a simple matter to get things done in Hayle.

Appendix

IMPORTS INTO HAYLE (excluding COAL) for the year 1815 from a Customs Sufferance Book with the permission of the late Miss A. G. D. La Touche.

From	No. of arrivals	Typical cargoes
Swansea	34	Earthenware, cheese, beer, oatmeal, chains, butter.
Bristol	14	Loose ironware, tobacco pipes, linen drapery, hosiery, copper, bar iron, tar, paint, chairs, vinegar, household furniture, mustard, corks, cheese, musco sugar, molasses, hats, stationery, yarn, beer, cider, sacking, bacon, glass bottles, lead, pitch, wrought iron, sheet iron, spelter, sailcloth, twines, cordage, ironware, hard soap, brandy, rum, gin, rum shrub, port wine, British spirits, tobacco, snuff, drugs, barrel staves, cast iron wheels.
Padstow	12	Oats, barley, wheat, malt, oak timber, scantle slates.
Bridgewater	9	Pantiles, ridge tiles, kiln tiles, bricks, elm timber, beans, peas, cheese, turneryware, chairs.
Chester	7	Fire tiles, fire bricks, bricks, cast iron rollers, earthenware.
London	7	Hemp, fir timber, rosin, lathwood, smelting pots, books, mats, glass, bunting, bone ash.
Newport	6	Pig iron, bar iron, bolt iron
Neath	5	Iron castings, oak timber, charcoal.
Bideford	4	Oats, barley.
Cardiff	3	Iron, nailrods, bar iron, bolt iron, iron castings.
Greenock	2	Copper, copper sheets, sheathing copper.
Liverpool	2	Wearing apparel, pipes, white salt.
Llanelly	2	Stamp heads, iron castings, fire bricks, Irish linen.
Exeter	2	Oak timber, cider.
Plymouth	2	Oak timber, oak staves, laths, old lead, cast iron and copper.
Cardigan	2	Oats.

113

EXPORTS FROM HAYLE for the year 1815

Destination	No. of departures	Copper ore (in tons)	Other cargoes
Swansea	180	12,577	Clay, tar, herrings pilchards.
Neath	55	2,963	
Llanelly	28	1,628	Clay.
Newport	12	580	Clay, blackjack, copper bolts, copper nails, copper sheets, copper bottoms, herrings.
Bristol	10	140	Manufactured copper, blackjack, coined tin, tin blocks, tin ingots, lead ore, copper boilers, copper nails, bush iron, old metal, old glass, old junk, paper, furniture, wearing apparel, pilchards, herrings.
Greenock	2		Manufactured copper.
Aberavon	1	160	
Bideford	1		Bone ash, books, wheat.
Cadiz	1		Potatoes.
Falmouth	1		Clay.
Liverpool	1		Manufactured copper.
Tenby	1		Norway deals.
Truro	1		Clay.
		18,048 tons	

The tonnages of the main exports, other than copper ore were:-

Clay	275 tons
Lead ore	10 tons
Manufactured copper	198 tons
Blackjack	43 tons
Iron	3 tons
Tin	233 blocks and 30 ingots

References

Abbreviations used:–

For newspapers

CM	*The Cornishman*
CT	*The Cornish Telegraph*
HT	*The Hayle Times*
Pz Gaz	*The Penzance Gazette*
RCG	*The Royal Cornwall Gazette*
SM	*The Sherborne Mercury*
WB	*The West Briton*
WMN	*The Western Morning News*

For other sources

DCNQ	*Devon & Cornwall Notes and Queries*
JRIC	*Journal of the Royal Institution of Cornwall*
JTS	*Journal of the Trevithick Society*
CRO	Cornwall Record Office, Truro
PRO	Public Record Office, Kew
RIC	Royal Institution of Cornwall, Truro

1   William Borlase, *The Natural History of Cornwall* 1758 pp.44-45

2   Ivor Thomas, *Cornishmen and Environment and the Isthmus of Penwith* 1947/8 p.22

3   RIC/Henderson Collection Calendar VI p.319

4   *WMN* 7 January 1974

5   W. H. Pascoe, *The History of the Cornish Copper Company* pp.159, 168

6   Edmund Vale, *The Harveys of Hayle* 1966 p.68

7   CRO DDH 1/181/37

8   *SM* 7 September 1779

9   *HT* 12 February 1960

10   CRO DDH 188/10

11   In possession of Lt. Cmdr. E. R. Coombe of Hayle in 1967

12   CRO DDWH 1735

13   CRO DDX 473/103h

14   CRO DDH 46/1-16 p.2119

15   ibid. p.975

16   PRO Close Rolls C54/6848 No.5

17   CRO DDH 46/1-16 p.2899
18   House of Commons Journal 1801, House of Lords Record Office
19   CRO DDX 473/103k
20   CRO DDX 473/1031
21   CRO DDX 473/100
22   CRO DDH 44
23   E. T. MacDermot, *History of the Great Western Railway* 1964
        Vol. II p.158
24   CRO DDH 207/33 West Cornwall Railway Bill 1847
25   William Borlase, *The Natural History of Cornwall* 1758 p.45
26   E. M. Philbrick, *The Redruth to Penzance Turnpike Roads, JTS* No.1
        1973 p.63 et seq
27   CM 20 July 1969
28   G. R. Anthony, *The Hayle, West Cornwall and Helston Railways* 1968
        p.10
29   *SM* 6 September 1779
30   *Robson's Commercial Directory* c.1839
31   Cyril Noall, *A History of the Cornish Mail and Stagecoaches* 1963 p.73
32   CRO DDH 207/28
33   ibid
34   Ivor Thomas, *Cornishmen and Environment and the Isthmus of Penwith*
        1947/8 p.21
35   ibid. p.60
36   Cyril Noall, *Cornish Lights and Shipwrecks* 1968 p.106
37   *Shipping Gazette*. Letter to the Editor dated 23 May 1838 from Wm.
        Sadler, Master of the barque *Sarah*
38   William Borlase, *The Natural History of Cornwall* 1758 pp.44-45
39   *Conveyancer Quarterly News* Winter Edn. 1958/9 p.6
40   *CT* 1 March 1871
41   Edmund Vale, *The Harveys of Hayle* 1966 p.329
42   CRO DDH 1/9/1-200
43   *CT* 2 February 1882
44   CRO DC/WPRDC 71
45   *JRIC* Vol. IV Pt.4 1964 p.388 et seq
46   William Borlase, *The Natural History of Cornwall* 1758 p.45
47   CRO DDWH 1780
48   Grahame Farr, *The Ships Register of the Port of Hayle* 1975 p.v
49   CRO DDH 1/181/36-39
50   CRO DDH 61

51 *WB* 6 May 1859
52 *Pz Gaz* 7 June 1843
53 *Pz Gaz* 7 December 1842
54 CRO DDH 207/28
55 ibid
56 *Pz Gaz* 3 February 1847
57 *WB* 2 November 1871
58 CRO DDH 71
59 *CT* 17 November 1887
60 *CT* 13 January 1887
61 *HT* 14 January 1955
62 *CT* 30 March 1882
63 R. M. Barton, *The Cornish China Clay Industry* 1966 p.125
64 *CT* 13 May 1879
65 *WB* 26 March 1883
66 CM 29 November 1883
67 CRO DDH 70
68 ibid
69 Clive Carter, *Trevithick Society Newsletter* No.10 August 1975 p.9 et seq
70 *WMN* 6 May 1960
71 *The History of Hayle*. A script to accompany an exhibition 1978 p.37
72 CM 29 November 1883
73 Edmund Vale, *The Harveys of Hayle* 1966 p.327
74 CRO DDH 1/181/36-39
75 *HT* 18 February 1955
76 Clive Carter, *Cornish Shipwrecks, The North Coast* 1978 p.88 et seq
77 Ivor Thomas, *Cornishmen and Environment and the Isthmus of Penwith* 1947/8 p.27
78 *JRIC* Vol. 8 1883 p.148
79 PRO SP 12/52
80 *JRIC* Vol. 4 1871/3 p.114
81 A. L. Rowse, *Tudor Cornwall* 1941 p.405
82 *Borlase Letter Book* No.1 April/July 1744 pp 51-87. At the Morrab Library, Penzance
83 *DCNQ* Vol. 27 p.143
84 D. B. Barton, *Essays in Cornish Mining History 2* 1971 p.134
85 *DCNQ* Vol. 27 p.329
86 Maurice H. Bizley, *Friendly Retreat* 1955 p.169

87   *CT* 3 October 1889
88   At the Westcountry Studies Library, Exeter
89   *CT* 28 September 1870
90   *JRIC* No.103 1966 p.187

Index